IN THE NAME OF

ALLAH

THE ALL-COMPASSIONATE, ALL-MERCIFUL

HAVING FUN
THE HALAL WAY
Entertainment in Islam

♦ **Title:** Having Fun the Halal Way – *Entertainment in Islam*

♦ **Author:** Abu Muawiyah Ismail Kamdar

♦ **English Edition 1 (2011)**

♦ **Layout Design:** Calix Ltd., Mauritius

♦ **Cover Design:** Sarwat Abbas

♦ **Filming:** Samo Press Group

HAVING FUN
THE HALAL WAY
Entertainment in Islam

اللهو المباح في الإسلام

Abu Muawiyah Ismail Kamdar

الدار العالمية للكتاب الإسلامي

INTERNATIONAL ISLAMIC PUBLISHING HOUSE

Copyright © 2011 International Islamic Publishing House
King Fahd National Library Cataloging-in-Publication Data

Abu Muawiyah Ismail Kamdar
   Having Fun the Halal Way – Entertainment in Islam. / Abu Muawiyah
   Ismail Kamdar. - Riyadh, 2011

   109 p ; 21 cm

   ISBN Paperback: 978-603-501-109-9

   1- Entertainment (Islamic ethics of)
   2- Amusement (Islamic ethics of)   3-Islamic ethics   I- Title

   212.7 dc   1432/5916

   Legal Deposit no. **1432/5916**
   ISBN Paperback: **978-603-501-109-9**

International Islamic Publishing House (IIPH)
P.O. Box 55195 Riyadh 11534, Saudi Arabia
Tel: 966 1 4650818/4647213 – Fax: 966 1 4633489
E-mail: iiph@iiph.com.sa – iiphsa@gmail.com
www.iiph.com.sa

Contents

Pronunciation and Transliteration Chart

Arabic script	Pronunciation	Transliterated form
أ	short 'a', as in *cat*	a
آ - ى	longer 'a', as in *cab* (not as in *cake*)	â
ب	/b/ as in *bell*, *rubber* and *tab*	b
ت	/t/ as in *tap*, *mustard* and *sit*	t
ة	takes the sound of the preceding diacritical mark sometimes ending in h (when in pausal form): ah, ih or ooh; or atu(n), ati(n) or ata(n) when uninterrupted	h or t (when followed by another Arabic word)
ث	/th/ as in *thing*, *maths* and *wealth*	th
ج	/j/ as in *jam*, *ajar* and *age*	j
ح	a 'harsher' sound than the English initial /h/, and may occur medially and in word-final position as well	ḥ
خ	as in *Bach* (in German); may occur initially and medially as well	kh

Arabic script	Pronunciation	Transliterated form
د	/d/ as in *do*, *muddy* and *red*	d
ذ	as in *this*, *father* and *smooth*	dh
ر	/r/ as in *raw*, *arid* and *war*; may also be a rolled 'r', as pronounced in Spanish	r
ز	/z/ as in *zoo*, *easy* and *gaze*	z
س	/s/ as in *so*, *messy* and *grass*	s
ش	as in *ship*, *ashes* and *rush*	sh
ص	no close equivalent in English, but may be approximated by pronouncing it as /sw/ or /s/ farther back in the mouth	ṣ
ض	no close equivalent in English, but may be approximated by pronouncing it as /d/ farther back in the mouth	ḍ
ط	no close equivalent in English, but may be approximated by pronouncing it as /t/ farther back in the mouth	t
ظ	no close equivalent in English, but may be approximated by pronouncing 'the' farther back in the mouth	d̲h̲
ع	no close equivalent in English: a guttural sound in the back of the throat	'
غ	no close equivalent in English, but may be closely approximated by pronouncing it like the French /r/ in 'rouge'	gh
ف	/f/ as in *fill*, *effort* and *muff*	f

Arabic script	Pronunciation	Transliterated form
ق	no close equivalent in English, but may be approximated by pronouncing it as /k/ farther back in the mouth	q
ك	/k/ as in *king*, *buckle* and *tack*	k
ل	/l/ as in *lap*, *halo*; in the word Allah, it becomes velarized as in *ball*	l
م	/m/ as in *men*, *simple* and *ram*	m
ن	/n/ as in *net*, *ant* and *can*	n
ه ـ ـه ـ ـهـ	/h/ as in *hat*; unlike /h/ in English, in Arabic /h/ is pronounced in medial and word-final positions as well	h
و	as in *wet* and *away*	w
و	long 'u', as in *boot* and *too*	oo
ي	as in *yard* and *mayo*	y
ي	long 'e', as in *eat*, *beef* and *see*	ee
ء	glottal stop: may be closely approximated by pronouncing it like 't' in the Cockney English pronunciation of *butter*: *bu'er*, or the stop sound in *uh-oh!*	(omitted in initial position)

Diphthongs

Arabic script	Pronunciation	Transliterated form
أو ، ـَو	long 'o', as in *owe*, *boat* and *go*	au, aw
أي ، ـَي	long 'a', as in *aid*, *rain* and *say*	ay, ai, ei

Diacritical marks (tashkeel)

Name of mark	Pronunciation	Transliterated form
Ō̇ fatḥah	very short 'a' or schwa (unstressed vowel)	a
Ọ̣ kasrah	shorter version of ee or schwa (unstressed vowel)	i
Ó ḍammah	shorter version of oo	u
Ő shaddah	a doubled consonant is stressed in the word, and the length of the sound is also doubled	double letter
Ő sukoon	no vowel sound between consonants or at the end of a word	absence of vowel

Arabic honorific symbols used in this book

(﷿): *Subḥânahu wa Ta'âla* — "The Exalted"

(ﷺ): *Ṣalla-Allâhu 'alayhi wa sallam* —   "Blessings and peace
be upon him"

(﷿): *'Alayhis-salâm* — "May peace be upon him"

(﷿): *Raḍiya-Allâhu 'anhu* — "May Allah be pleased with him"

(﷿): *Raḍiya-Allâhu 'anhâ* — "May Allah be pleased with her"

About the Word *Lord*

*T*he word *lord* in English has several related meanings. The original meaning is 'master' or 'ruler', and in this sense it is often used to refer to human beings: 'the *lord* of the mansion' or 'Lord So-and-So' (in the United Kingdom, for example). The word *Lord* with a capital L is used in the lexicon of Islam to refer to the One and Only God – Allah. In Islam, there is no ambiguity about the meaning of this word. While it is true that one may occasionally use the word *lord* (whether capitalized or not) to refer to a human being, in Islamic discourse the reference of this term is always clear from the context. Whereas for Christians, Hindus and other polytheists, the word *Lord* with a capital L may refer to Allah, to Jesus or to some imagined deity, for Muslims, there can be no plurality of meaning. Allah alone is the Lord, and the Lord is Allah – not Jesus, not Rama, not any other being.

The Editor

Publisher's Note

*A*ll praise and thanks belong to Allah alone, the One, the Almighty and All-Merciful. Blessings and peace be upon Prophet Muhammad, the last of His Messengers and Prophets, and upon his family, his Companions and all those who follow in his footsteps until the end of time.

The concept of entertainment is rather unclear in the minds of most of the Muslims. On one hand, there are aspects that are clearly forbidden, but on the other hand, there are avenues that can be explored by those looking for some permissible means of recreation.

In *Having Fun the Halal Way*, Ismail Kamdar has explained, in detail, the exact stance of Islam with regard to entertainment. He has clearly identified areas that are out-of-bounds for practicing Muslims; also, he has specified activities that they can enjoy in their leisure time.

We hope that the suggestions in this book will enable the reader to clearly assess his or her pursuit of recreational activities and use the guidelines given here to take a balanced approach of the subject of entertainment.

May Allah accept the efforts of all those who have contributed to the production of this book, and may it be acceptable to Him, *âmeen.*

Muhammad Abdul Mohsin Al-Tuwaijri
Managing Director
International Islamic Publishing House
Riyadh, Saudi Arabia

Introduction

All praise is due to Allah (*Subḥânahu wa Ta'âlâ* – Glorified and Exalted is He), who has legislated for us a religion which is balanced and easy to practise. May His peace and blessings descend upon His final messenger, the mercy to the universe, Muhammad (*ṣalla Allâhu 'alayhi wa sallam* – blessings and peace be upon him) and all those who follow his way until the last day.

We live in a time in which, for many people, entertainment has become the most important aspect of life. Indeed, it would not be too far-fetched to state that many people today worship entertainment and entertainers. The music, television and movie industries are the highest generators of income for many leading countries; the actors and singers involved are worshipped by many in a very literal sense.

It is for this reason, among others, that it is important for Muslims to be well-acquainted with the Islamic stance on entertainment in its various forms, so that they are able to cope with this situation. There is, however, another important reason for my having chosen to research and write about this topic.

In light of the current entertainment culture (commonly called pop culture), many Muslim parents find themselves in a dilemma regarding their children's access to entertainment. In general, two extremes have developed and been adopted, both of which lead to negative results.

The first extreme is of those who are overawed by the technological progress of the West and disheartened by the failure of Muslims in this area (and in all justice, we have been a failure in this area). This low self-esteem has led Muslims to embrace the Western entertainment-oriented lifestyle completely, so much so that it is not unusual to find Muslim homes with multiple television sets and video game machines, with no restrictions as to what kind of movies, songs or games are played. This is common in the homes of many who are ignorant of Islamic laws, suffering from low self-esteem, or simply very hedonistic in their lifestyles.

The negative effect of this is all too obvious, and one can see the repercussions everywhere. Muslims become brainwashed by the media to such an extent that it becomes impossible to distinguish them from the disbelievers. Muhammad Salih al-Munajjid has commented on the effect of raising children in this manner:

> I also know of people at the other extreme, who refuse to get involved in their children's affairs at all, claiming that the child will not be convinced that a mistake is a mistake or a sin is a sin unless he does it and then finds out for himself that it is a mistake. This deviant idea comes from being weaned on ideas of western philosophy and notions of absolute freedom. Some of them give their child free rein, fearing that the child may start to hate them, saying: I will earn his love whatever he does. Some of them give the child free rein as a reaction to their own over-strict upbringings, thinking that they have to do the absolute opposite with their own children. Some of them take this stupid attitude to extremes by saying: Let our sons and daughters enjoy their youth as they wish. Do these people not think that their children might pull on their clothes

on the Day of Resurrection and say: O my father, why did you leave me in sin?[1]

Such Muslims are busy with television, video games, movies, music and sports. They are also engrossed in earning money in order to indulge in such things, to the extent that they have no time to even think about Allah (﷽) or Islam, let alone study or practise their religion. Allah (﷽) has described such a state in many places in the Qur'an, such as:

﴿ أَلۡهَٮٰكُمُ ٱلتَّكَاثُرُ ۝ حَتَّىٰ زُرۡتُمُ ٱلۡمَقَابِرَ ۝ كَلَّا سَوۡفَ تَعۡلَمُونَ ۝ ثُمَّ كَلَّا سَوۡفَ تَعۡلَمُونَ ۝ كَلَّا لَوۡ تَعۡلَمُونَ عِلۡمَ ٱلۡيَقِينِ ۝ لَتَرَوُنَّ ٱلۡجَحِيمَ ۝ ثُمَّ لَتَرَوُنَّهَا عَيۡنَ ٱلۡيَقِينِ ۝ ثُمَّ لَتُسۡـَٔلُنَّ يَوۡمَئِذٍ عَنِ ٱلنَّعِيمِ ۝ ﴾

(تكاثر: الآية ١ – ٨)

❨Competition in [worldly] increase diverts you, until you visit the graveyards. No! You are going to know. Then no! You are going to know. No! If you only knew with knowledge of certainty, you will surely see the hellfire. Then you will surely see it with the eye of certainty. Then you will surely be asked that day about pleasure.❩

(Qur'an 102: 1-8)[2]

The other extreme is of those who fear Allah (﷽) but, due to ignorance or blind following of certain schools of thought or scholars, have totally rejected the idea of entertainment. Indeed, it is human nature to completely turn away from something which appears to be a cause of great evil. However, this hatred for entertainment has been taken by some to an unnatural extreme, which has had negative psychological effects on the youth and children raised in such households.

The youngsters in such homes are prohibited from enjoying any form of entertainment, whether inside the house or outside.

They are taught that they should spend all their time worshipping Allah (﷽), since that is what humans have been created for. (It is, indeed, the purpose of our creation; however, Allah (﷽) has legislated for us a balanced religion). This is an unnatural state, similar to that of monks and their monasticism. All human beings have a natural desire to enjoy themselves and have fun. If such desires are overly suppressed, they can push an individual over the edge. I have often observed that such suppression leads to the youngsters becoming rebellious and turning to the worst forms of entertainment to try and satisfy their suppressed desires. One can routinely come across youths who hail from practising Muslim homes, yet who smoke, take drugs and are addicted to pornography.

Such observations clearly elucidate the need for and importance of a book on this topic. If we want to overcome the entertainment revolution without going to an unnatural extreme, we will have to learn and understand the true teachings of Islam regarding it. Islam is a complete way of life, which guides us on every issue. It is an easy and balanced religion, well in tune with our *fiṭrah* (the natural inclination instilled by Allah). One should not be surprised to find that the Islamic view on entertainment is practical, easy to follow, and balanced between the aforementioned two extremes.

I ask Allah (﷽) to guide me in writing this, to accept it and make it a means of guidance and benefit for others. I beseech Him to forgive me for any mistakes herein. I thank Allah (﷽) for allowing me to complete this book, and I thank all those people who assisted me in doing so: Dr Abu Ameenah Bilal Philips and Sister Umm Yusuf for assisting me with the editing, and my wife Farzana for her support, advice and encouragement. Everything good in this book is from Allah (﷽); all the mistakes therein are from me or the devil. Verily, only Allah (﷽) is all-perfect and free from making mistakes.

Chapter One

Some basic principles of fiqh (Islamic jurisprudence)

Before delving into the topic at hand, it is important to clarify a few basic principles that I have used to formulate my opinions mentioned in this book. The first point I wish to make is that this book will definitely have either mistakes or points that you may not agree with. Indeed, it is impossible to delve into the area of fiqh and not make mistakes. However, qualified scholars or students of knowledge who are sincere, follow the general principles, and struggle to find the right answer, will be rewarded even if the final conclusion is wrong. If they later discover or are made aware of a mistake, though, they must immediately publicly retract the earlier mistaken position and state clearly the corrected view.

'Amr ibn al-'Âṣ (*raḍiya Allâhu 'anhu* – may Allah be pleased with him) narrated that he heard the Prophet (ﷺ) say: « If a judge passes judgement, having striven to reach a decision, and he gets it right, he will have two rewards. If he passes judgement, having striven to reach a decision, and he gets it wrong, he will have one reward. » (Muslim)

This is why it is not permissible to blindly follow anyone other than the Prophet (ﷺ), especially when one knows that the person he or she is following is wrong. Every scholar makes mistakes, so one should try to follow the best opinion on an issue and not cling to the view of one's *madh-hab* (school of juristic thought) or *shaykh* (teacher or scholar). Of course, it is permissible to follow the ruling of a scholar that you trust in an area where you lack knowledge, until you become knowledgeable enough to decide for yourself. This is why I say that it is not permissible for anybody to blindly follow my opinions on specific issues in this book. I invite them to research the discussed issues further if they feel my evidence is not strong enough.

This leads me to my next point: the method I will be using in this book will be that of the righteous predecessors. I am not biased towards or against any madh-hab or scholar. The rulings here are based on the sources of Islamic law using the principles of fiqh. Any differences in the schools of thought will be discussed in light of the evidence.

Sources of Islamic law

The agreed-upon sources of Islamic law are as follows, in the order presented:

1) The Qur'an

2) The *Sunnah* (the practice and collected sayings of Prophet Muhammad)

The Qur'an and Sunnah go hand in hand. The Sunnah explains the general rulings in the Qur'an, thus making them specific. It must be noted that, in Islamic law, the Sunnah is regarded as having weight equal to the Qur'an since both are Allah's revelation; as such, any ruling mentioned in either must be submitted to and obeyed by all the Muslims. In *Sharia* (Islamic law), the Sunnah complements the Qur'an and cannot be used as a replacement for the Qur'an. Similarly, deriving a verdict by referring to the words of the Qur'an without cross-checking it by reference to the explanation of the Qur'an through authentic *hadiths* (statements or action of Prophet Muhammad that were remembered and recorded by his Companions and followers) is wrong. I mention this because, with regard to many issues that will be discussed in this book, the argument of some ignorant people is: "But it is just a hadith; it does not appear in the Qur'an." This argument is baseless in Islam, as Allah (ﷺ) has commanded us:

﴿ ... وَمَآ ءَاتَىٰكُمُ ٱلرَّسُولُ فَخُذُوهُ وَمَا نَهَىٰكُمْ عَنْهُ فَٱنتَهُواْ ... ۞ ﴾

(سورة حشر: الآية ٧)

﴿...And whatever the Messenger has given you – take; and what he has forbidden you – refrain from...﴾   *(Qur'an 59: 7)*

3) *Ijmâ'* (scholarly consensus)

Any issue upon which the scholars among the Companions of the Prophet (ﷺ) agreed is binding upon us. They lived with the Prophet (ﷺ) and understood Islam best, so if they agreed upon a ruling, it has to be correct. This is supported by the following hadith:

The Prophet (ﷺ) said: « My nation will not unite on misguidance... » (Recorded by Ibn Mâjah and aṭ-Ṭabarâni with a sound chain of narrators)

4) *Qiyâs* (analogy)

If a ruling cannot be deduced from the aforementioned three sources, Islam has allowed deduction based on the principles extracted from these same sources. An example of this would be the prohibition of smoking cigarettes. There is no Qur'anic verse or hadith that states that smoking is prohibited. However, Allah (ﷺ) tells us:

(سورة البقرة: الآية ١٩٥)   ﴿ ... وَلَا تُلْقُوا بِأَيْدِيكُمْ إِلَى ٱلتَّهْلُكَةِ ... ﴾

❨...do not throw [yourselves] with your [own] hands into destruction...❩   *(Qur'an 2: 195)*

Also, there are many hadiths that instruct the Muslims to avoid all those things which might harm them. Considering these, and the fact that smoking is extremely harmful and a cause of cancer and death, scholars have deduced that smoking cigarettes is prohibited.

These are the four agreed-upon sources of Islamic law. Of course, there are many other sources, but the scholars differ in the acceptability of their usage, so we shall stick to these four.

Basic Principles

There are certain basic principles that are used when deducing Islamic rulings; I will mention here only those principles that are relevant to our topic.

It is important, however, to first make a distinction between Sharia and fiqh, both of which are often translated into English as 'Islamic law'. Sharia refers to the main body of laws clearly mentioned in the Qur'an and Sunnah, which are fixed and agreed upon. These laws are unchangeable because the nature of human beings is constant. Hence, the basic duties of a human will never change. Laws that fall into this category include the command to fulfil the five pillars of Islam and the prohibition of fornication, adultery and homosexuality.

Fiqh refers to secondary laws for which Allah (ﷻ), in His infinite mercy, has left only general guidelines. Scholars differ regarding these laws; they are quite flexible and can change according to circumstances. The wisdom behind this is to ensure that, through fiqh, Islam remains flexible and applicable in all eras and cultures.

Islam recognises that even though humans do not change, their cultures, circumstances and technological levels do change. Hence, Allah (🌸) has left these areas with general guidelines which we operate under. It is these guidelines that the scholars refer to as the principles of fiqh. Some of the principles that concern us here are as follows:

1. The general principle in Islam regarding the things of this world (including entertainment) is that everything is *halâl* (permitted according to Islamic law) unless proven *harâm* (forbidden according to Islamic law). Regarding acts of worship, it is the opposite; everything is *bid'ah* (undesirable innovation) and harâm unless proven to be permissible. Based on this principle, one must bear in mind that a form of entertainment can be declared prohibited only if there is substantial evidence from the Qur'an or Sunnah.

   There are many proofs from which this principle has been deduced, including the following explicit hadith:

   The Prophet (🌸) said: « The lawful is that which Allah (🌸) has made lawful for you, and the prohibited is that which is prohibited in His Book; that concerning which He is silent, He has permitted as a mercy to you. » (Bukhari, Ibn Mâjah and at-Tirmidhi)

   By default, every worldly action is permissible unless one finds sufficient evidence to prove that it is prohibited.

2. Anything that distracts a person from his or her religious duties is harâm. Using this principle, playing soccer is considered halâl, but if it leads a person to miss the prayers, dress in an unsuitable manner or use offensive language, it becomes harâm for that individual. This is an example of how a fiqh ruling can vary from person to person.

A proof of this is in a chapter in the Qur'an called *at-Takâthur* (Rivalry in worldly increase):

$$ ﴿ أَلۡهَىٰكُمُ ٱلتَّكَاثُرُ ۞ حَتَّىٰ زُرۡتُمُ ٱلۡمَقَابِرَ ۞ ﴾ $$

(سورة تكاثر: الآية ١ – ٢)

❨Competition in [worldly] increase diverts you, until you visit the graveyards.❩   *(Qur'an 102: 1-2)*

Ibn Qayyim points out that Allah (ﷻ) uses the word 'divert' and not 'busy' because it is possible for a person to be busy with the world but still remember Allah (ﷻ). However, when the permissible things of this world become a distraction from Allah (ﷻ), they become harâm, and this verse applies to such a situation.[3]

3. There are five categories of actions according to fiqh. These are: *fard* (compulsory), *sunnah* (recommended), *mubâh* (permissible), *makrooh* (disliked) and *harâm* (prohibited). I will, therefore, attempt to place each form of entertainment into one of these categories. A person only falls into sin by doing something that is harâm or neglecting something that is fard.

4. The Sharia aims to preserve five things: Religion (meaning Islam), life, intellect, the human race and the economy. Any form of entertainment that affects any of these in a negative manner would generally be categorised as harâm. On the other hand, if it benefits any of them, then it would be categorised as sunnah as long as it has no traces of harâm.

5. Anything without value or benefit is regarded as a waste of time. Such a thing is not harâm in itself; however, it can become harâm if one indulges in it excessively. Generally, things that waste time are regarded as makrooh.

Muhammad Salih al-Munajjid gives the following advice regarding entertainment for children:

Make sure that your children's play is both entertaining and purposeful. Give them a special playroom, or at least a cupboard for their toys, where they can keep their toys tidy. Avoid toys that go against *shari'ah*, like musical instruments, or toys that have crosses or them, or games containing dice.[4]

6. Scholars sometimes extract multiple rulings from one hadith. Therefore, some hadiths are quoted more than once in this book, when they are relevant to more than one topic.

There are many other principles and important issues that one should learn concerning the nature and history of fiqh; however, that is not the topic of this book.

Chapter Two

The Western concept of entertainment

*B*efore discussing the rulings on specific forms of entertainment, it is important that we understand the Islamic and Western concepts of entertainment and its place in both ways of life.

Entertainment can be defined as an activity designed to give people a diversion. Entertainment tends to be passive; certain forms of entertainment which involve active participation, like reading and engaging in sports, belong to a subcategory known as recreation.

It is important to note that human beings have been discovering various avenues to entertain themselves throughout history. The idea of enjoying oneself with a diversion from the mundane is part of human nature and has always existed. Although it is a natural trait, humans tend to go to extremes in fulfilling their desires. We find various examples of this trend in the modern Western entertainment industry.

The entertainment industry has reached a peak in the modern world unlike in any previous period in history. The content is so diverse that it is possible for people to entertain themselves almost continuously for years on end, and we find people increasingly moving in this direction. Addiction to television, movies, video games and music is commonplace. People walk with their headphones connected to their iPods, PlayStation portables (PSPs) and other portable forms of entertainment. Indeed, many people today live for entertainment.

This boom in the entertainment industry has two main causes. The first of these is the advancement of technology in recent history, hence allowing humans to create previously unimaginable forms of entertainment. The second is the Western ideology of life itself. In fact, the average Westerner, under the banner of secular democracy (meaning rule by the people, without interference from religion), has been raised to believe that one's purpose in life is only to enjoy oneself. The commonly-quoted saying, "You only live once, so make the most of it," means that one should enjoy this world as much as possible, since there is no second chance.

This ideology will undoubtedly cause people to live their lives for entertainment. Thus, the goal of the average Westerner is to enjoy life with every possible form of entertainment and to make as much money as possible in order to acquire more expensive forms of entertainment. Their goal is essentially entertainment, and the means towards such a goal is to make money. Thus, one can say that the most commonly worshipped idols on earth today are money and entertainment. Allah (ﷻ) says in the Qur'an:

﴿ أَرَءَيْتَ مَنِ ٱتَّخَذَ إِلَٰهَهُۥ هَوَىٰهُ أَفَأَنتَ تَكُونُ عَلَيْهِ وَكِيلاً ۝ ﴾

(سورة فرقان: الآية ٤٣)

⟪Have you seen the one who takes as his god his own desire? Then would you be responsible for him?⟫   *(Qur'an 25: 43)*

Since such people believe in secularism, they have divorced religion from their lives. As a result, all the moral boundaries in the way of attaining such a goal are discarded. The result is what we see today: people are willing to go to any means necessary to earn money. They are inventing various forms of entertainment with no moral limits. This has led to the spread of such evils as pornography, homosexuality, casual sex and many other open vices.

When we explore the Islamic view of entertainment, the problems with the Western concept will become clear; however, I wish to draw the reader's attention to certain verses in the Qur'an which describe the lifestyle of the disbeliever exactly as mentioned above. This shows the relevance of the Qur'an to every day and age; this is part of the miraculous nature of the Qur'an. It is the right of Allah (﷾) that every human studies and ponders the Qur'an, so that its guidance can become manifest in our lives.

﴿ وَمَا ٱلْحَيَوٰةُ ٱلدُّنْيَآ إِلَّا لَعِبٌ وَلَهْوٌ ۖ وَلَلدَّارُ ٱلْأَخِرَةُ خَيْرٌ لِّلَّذِينَ يَتَّقُونَ ۗ أَفَلَا تَعْقِلُونَ ۝ ﴾ (سورة أنعام: الآية ٣٢)

⟪And the worldly life is not but amusement and diversion; but the home of the hereafter is best for those who fear Allah (﷾), so will you not reason?⟫ *(Qur'an 6: 32)*

In this verse, Allah (﷾) has informed us that those who centre their lives around Him will have the best of the afterlife. At the same time, He has explained what people who shun Allah (﷾) do with their time: nothing but entertainment. Allah (﷾) then invites us to think about this and to ask ourselves: do we understand that paradise is far greater than this world? Is it sensible to exchange the greatest of Allah's gifts, an eternal life of fun and entertainment in paradise, for something which is insignificant in comparison to it? Indeed, only a fool allows oneself to be distracted from Allah (﷾) and paradise by the temporary enjoyments of this world.

﴿ ٱلَّذِينَ ٱتَّخَذُواْ دِينَهُمْ لَهْوًا وَلَعِبًا وَغَرَّتْهُمُ ٱلْحَيَوٰةُ ٱلدُّنْيَا ۚ فَٱلْيَوْمَ نَنسَىٰهُمْ كَمَا نَسُواْ لِقَآءَ يَوْمِهِمْ هَٰذَا وَمَا كَانُواْ بِـَٔايَٰتِنَا يَجْحَدُونَ ۝ ﴾

(سورة الأعراف: الآية ٥١)

❨Who took their religion as distraction and amusement and whom the worldly life deluded. So today We will forget them just as they forgot the meeting of this day of theirs and for having rejected Our verses.❩   *(Qur'an 7: 51)*

This verse is a stern warning to all those people who ignore Allah (ﷻ) and indulge themselves in this world. In fact, in this verse, Allah (ﷻ) calls entertainment their *deen* (religion or way of life), showing that some people will indeed make entertainment their goal in life as we see today. Such people will be ignored by Allah (ﷻ) in the afterlife. They will be in the hellfire where they will scream for help, but nobody will care to respond since they ignored their duties to Allah (ﷻ) in this life. We ask Allah (ﷻ) to save us from being among them.

These are just two of many verses in the Qur'an which condemn this lifestyle and, likewise, its miserable end. Indeed, we were created for a much greater purpose than to just indulge ourselves in this world, as will be explained in the next chapter.

Chapter Three

The Islamic view
of entertainment

$\mathscr{A}$s Muslims, we know that there is much more to life than enjoyment and diversions. In fact, Allah (﷽) tells us in the Qur'an:

﴿ وَمَا خَلَقْنَا ٱلسَّمَآءَ وَٱلْأَرْضَ وَمَا بَيْنَهُمَا لَـٰعِبِينَ ۞ ﴾   (سورة الأنبياء: الآية ١٦)

❮And We did not create the heaven and earth and that between them in play.❯ *(Qur'an 21: 16)*

If we humans cannot even manufacture the smallest of things without a reason or purpose, it is ludicrous to believe that Allah (﷽) would create this entire universe without any purpose or reason.

Allah (﷽) clearly tells us in the Qur'an:

﴿ وَمَا خَلَقْتُ ٱلْجِنَّ وَٱلْإِنسَ إِلَّا لِيَعْبُدُونِ ۞ ﴾   (سورة ذاريات: الآية ٥٦)

❮And I did not create the jinn and mankind except to worship Me.❯ *(Qur'an 51: 56)*

Thus, our purpose in life is clear: to worship Allah Almighty (﷽). He has given us a free will, so we worship by choice.

If we fulfil our divine purpose, He will reward us with paradise. If we ignore it, He will cast us into hellfire, just as we cast our useless items into the garbage dump. Allah (ﷻ) does not need us; rather, we need Him and His mercy.

However, before I move on, it is important that we understand what is meant here by worship. In Islam, worship is a broad term which is not restricted to rituals. The Arabic word for worship here is *'ibâdah,* which can also be translated as servitude or slavery. This means that we are supposed to behave on earth as slaves of Allah (ﷻ), doing what He wants and staying away from all that displeases Him. Another word that can be used to describe our duty to Allah (ﷻ) is the word 'Islam' itself, which can be translated as 'surrender and submission to the will of Allah (ﷻ)'. This understanding is important because it shows us that we do not have to pray all day to fulfil our purpose in life. Rather, if we live our lives within the boundaries set by Allah (ﷻ), fulfilling our obligations towards Him and staying away from His prohibitions, with the intention to please Him, our every act becomes an 'ibâdah (act of worship)! For instance, our sleep can be an act of worship, our eating can be an act of worship, and even entertaining ourselves within the boundaries of Islam can be an act of worship. This is the correct understanding of our purpose in life.

If our purpose in life is to worship Allah (ﷻ), how does entertainment fit into the equation? Should we not be serious all the time, worried about the afterlife and praying to Allah (ﷻ)? If we were doing so, it would be the ideal scenario. There would be no difference between us and the angels. However, Allah (ﷻ) has created humans with different needs and defined the boundaries within which they can fulfil them. One such need is for entertainment or recreation. True Muslims spend their time wisely, doing only what pleases Allah (ﷻ). However, wise Muslims know how to maintain balance in life. They know that if they do not take a break every now and then, to rest and enjoy Allah's blessings, this can lead to negative results such as losing their energy, being unable to continue in their worship or even developing a mental illness. Wise believers take breaks from their daily worship to enjoy some of the things which Allah (﷾) has made permissible, with the intention of recharging their energy levels in order to worship Allah (﷾) even better. Following this logic, entertaining oneself in a permissible manner becomes an act of worship and is rewarded.

One should note, though, that even without that intention, entertaining oneself with something permissible is not frowned upon in Islam if done in moderation. However, Ibn Qayyim has pointed out that to reach the higher levels of piety, one should voluntarily stay away from the permissible but futile actions and instead involve oneself with those that bring rewards.[5] It is not permissible to force this abstinence on others, though, since this is something that should be done voluntarily; all humans differ in their levels of piety and worldly needs.

The Islamic concept of entertainment is that it is a natural human desire which can be fulfilled within the boundaries of Allah (﷾), but it is not the sole goal or purpose of a Muslim in and of itself. Here we note a few differences between our understanding of entertainment and that of the West. Firstly, for Muslims, entertainment is not a goal in itself; it is a blessing from Allah (﷾) to be enjoyed. Secondly, entertainment in Islam has limits set by Allah (﷾), which must be firmly adhered to.

These factors distinguish between the practising Muslim and the average Westerner. Both entertain themselves, yet a Muslim earns numerous rewards for obeying Allah (﷾), while a Westerner incurs the wrath of Allah (﷾) by forgetting Him and crossing the limits of permissible entertainment. The difference is vast because it involves the purpose of existence itself.

I will now state some general proofs for the permissibility of entertaining oneself and enjoying all that is allowed. This is especially for the benefit of those who, in their ignorance, go to the extreme of declaring most, if not all, forms of entertainment to be forbidden, making Islam difficult for themselves and others.

1. There is a principle in Islam that states that following the religion is easy. Scholars of Islam have agreed that the general principle is that everything is permissible unless proven otherwise. Hence, the burden of proof actually falls on those who say entertainment is prohibited. The following verses prove this principle:

﴿ ... يُرِيدُ ٱللَّهُ بِكُمُ ٱلْيُسْرَ وَلَا يُرِيدُ بِكُمُ ٱلْعُسْرَ... ۝ ﴾

(سورة البقرة: الآية ١٨٥)

﴿...Allah intends for you ease and does not intend for you hardship...﴾   *(Qur'an 2: 185)*

﴿ ... وَمَا جَعَلَ عَلَيْكُمْ فِى ٱلدِّينِ مِنْ حَرَجٍ ... ۝ ﴾

(سورة حج: الآية ٧٨)

﴿...has not placed upon you in the religion any difficulty...﴾   *(Qur'an 22: 78)*

The following hadith also proves this principle:

The Prophet (ﷺ) said: « Religion is very easy, and whoever overburdens himself in his religion will not be able to continue in that way. So you should not be extremists, but aim to be near to perfection and receive the good tidings that you will be rewarded; and gain strength by worshipping in the mornings and the nights. » (Bukhari)

In fact, Imam Bukhari named a chapter in his *Ṣaḥeeḥ al-Bukhâri*: "The chapter of the religion being easy." It contains more evidence to prove this point.

2. Islam condemns those who prohibit the good things of this world without any proof. Allah (ﷺ) has said:

﴿ قُلْ مَنْ حَرَّمَ زِينَةَ ٱللَّهِ ٱلَّتِيٓ أَخْرَجَ لِعِبَادِهِۦ وَٱلطَّيِّبَٰتِ مِنَ ٱلرِّزْقِ قُلْ هِيَ لِلَّذِينَ ءَامَنُوا۟ فِى ٱلْحَيَوٰةِ ٱلدُّنْيَا خَالِصَةً يَوْمَ ٱلْقِيَٰمَةِ كَذَٰلِكَ نُفَصِّلُ ٱلْأَيَٰتِ لِقَوْمٍ يَعْلَمُونَ ۝ قُلْ إِنَّمَا حَرَّمَ رَبِّىَ ٱلْفَوَٰحِشَ مَا ظَهَرَ مِنْهَا وَمَا بَطَنَ وَٱلْإِثْمَ وَٱلْبَغْىَ بِغَيْرِ ٱلْحَقِّ وَأَن تُشْرِكُوا۟ بِٱللَّهِ مَا لَمْ يُنَزِّلْ بِهِۦ سُلْطَٰنًا وَأَن تَقُولُوا۟ عَلَى ٱللَّهِ مَا لَا تَعْلَمُونَ ۝ ﴾

(سورة الأعراف: الآية ٣٢ – ٣٣)

❪Say: Who has forbidden the adornment of [from] Allah which He has produced for His servants and the good [lawful] things of provision? Say: They are for those who believe during worldly life [but] exclusively for them on the Day of Resurrection. Thus do We detail the verses for a people who know. Say: My Lord has only forbidden immoralities – what is apparent of them and what is concealed – and sin, and oppression without right, and that you associate with Allah that for which He has not sent down authority, and that you say about Allah that which you do not know.❫ *(Qur'an 7: 32-33)*

3. The Prophet (ﷺ) did not disapprove when his Companions (may Allah be pleased with them) enjoyed themselves with permissible activities. The following hadith is a good example:

« It has been narrated by 'Â'ishah (*radiya Allâhu 'anhâ* – may Allah be pleased with her), the wife of the Prophet, that once the Prophet Muhammad (ﷺ) came home, and at that time, two little girls were singing songs about the battle of Bu'âth.[6] The Prophet (ﷺ) lay down on the bed and turned his face away. Then Abu Bakr (&) came and scolded her, saying: These musical instruments of Satan in the house of the Prophet of Allah (&)! Prophet Muhammad turned to him and said: Leave them. In the words of 'Â'ishah (&): When Abu Bakr got busy in other matters, I told the two girls to leave, and they left. That was the day of [the Islamic celebration of] *Eid*. The Abyssinians were playing in the mosque with shields and lances. Then either I asked the Messenger (&), or he himself said: Do you want to have a look? I said yes, so he let me stand behind him, with my cheek against his cheek, and said: Carry on, Banu Arfidah. When I became bored, he asked: Is that enough for you? I said yes. He said: Then you may leave. » (Bukhari)

From this hadith, it is clear that the Prophet (&) saw nothing wrong with his Companions entertaining themselves with innocent songs accompanied by a hand-drum, or by playing. He disapproved of Abu Bakr (&) censuring them and instead allowed them to continue. This hadith will play an important role in later discussions in this book.

« While some Ethiopians were playing in the presence of the Prophet (&), 'Umar (&) came in, picked up a stone and hit them with it. Seeing that, the Prophet (&) said: O 'Umar! Allow them [to play]. Ma'mar [the sub-narrator] added that they were playing in the mosque. » (Bukhari)

The Prophet (&) once told a young Companion who had married an older, previously-married woman: « Why haven't you married a virgin who would have played with you, and you would have played with her? » (Bukhari)

4. Islam is the religion of the fiṭrah of human beings. As such, it caters to every natural need of theirs, which includes the need for leisure and entertainment.

As we progress and discuss other narrations, it will become clearer to the reader that Islam caters to a human's needs in many ways, and there is a lot of scope for enjoying the good things of this life.

A misunderstood hadith

The Prophet (ﷺ) said: « Any act of entertainment done by a believer is void (*bâṭil*) except three: playing with one's family, training a horse and practicing shooting. » (A reliable hadith recorded by Aḥmad and at-Tirmidhi)

This narration is often misquoted to prove that all forms of entertainment and leisure, except three, are void. In this regard, one should note, firstly, that scholars have differed over the authenticity of this hadith. Secondly, this is a gross misinterpretation; there is nothing in the wording of the hadith that says that everything else is ḥarâm. It simply states that everything else is bâṭil (void/useless), which means one is not rewarded for entertaining oneself except with one of the three mentioned types, or if one indulges in any other form of permissible entertainment while remembering Allah (ﷻ). Allah (ﷻ) knows best.

Imam al-Ghazâli has said regarding this hadith:

> The Prophet (ﷺ) saying that these things are void does not indicate prohibition, rather it indicates lack of benefit, and it is authentically reported that the Prophet (ﷺ) enjoyed watching the Abyssinians playing with their spears in the masjid which is not one of these three things.[7]

Chapter Four

Prohibited forms of entertainment

In this chapter, we will discuss those forms of entertainment that are clearly prohibited, or harâm, in Islam. We will also delve into disputed issues like the use of musical instruments. The purpose of this is to clarify the things one should avoid. Knowing this, one can work out what is permissible, since the prohibited forms are few, while those which Allah (ﷻ) has allowed are many.

Anything involving or promoting *shirk* (associating partners with Allah) or *kufr* (disbelief)

The greatest sin that a human can commit is to give the exclusive rights of Allah (ﷻ) to anyone other than Him. This is known as shirk, and it can take many forms.[8]

We will discuss here only those forms of shirk and kufr that are often viewed as harmless forms of entertainment, the most common of which is real magic (*sihr*). Islam has condemned magic very staunchly; in fact, the Qur'an has declared as a disbeliever every person who learns magic. Allah (ﷻ) has said:

‫) ... وَمَا كَفَرَ سُلَيْمَنُ وَلَكِنَّ ٱلشَّيَطِينَ كَفَرُواْ يُعَلِّمُونَ ٱلنَّاسَ ٱلسِّحْرَ ...‬ ﴾ ⚅ ﴿

(‫سورة البقرة: الآية ١٠٢‬)

《...It was not Solomon who disbelieved, but the devils disbelieved, teaching people magic...》   *(Qur'an 2: 102)*

The Islamic punishment for magicians and sorcerers is execution by the sword. Since magic is hated in Islam and regarded as kufr, watching and enjoying someone else performing magic would be, at the very least, a sin; some scholars argue that it is also a form of kufr. Note that the above refers only to sihr and does not include illusionary tricks such as those done with cards and ropes. Dr. Muzammil Siddiqi, former president of the Islamic Society of North America (ISNA), answered a question at the Islamonline.net website about 'magic shows' by saying:

> The word 'magic' has many definitions in English language. It could mean 'black magic' which may include sorcery, amulets, talismans, potions, charms, spells exorcism etc. But it could also mean just a sleight of hands used for entertainment. The 'magic shows' generally belong to this last category and I do not think doing such acts for the purpose of entertainment is *haraam* or *makruh* in Islam...

> Magic in this sense or *sihr*, witchcraft, oracles, palmistry, fortune telling etc. are all forbidden or *haraam* in Islam.

> However, mere tricks for entertainment purposes should not be called *sihr* in the classical sense. Through these shows we can teach our children that they should not be deceived by illusions. Some people may use the sleight of their hands and make them believe that they control supernatural powers. Children should be aware of those characters and should not be naive to believe such people.

Another form of shirk that is being practiced as entertainment nowadays is fortune telling. The Prophet (ﷺ) said: « Whoever visits a fortune-teller and believes him has disbelieved in what has been revealed to Muhammad. » (Bukhari and Abu Dâwood)

It is an act of kufr to believe a fortune-teller. It is tantamount to shirk because one believes the fortune-teller to possess one of the attributes of Allah (ﷻ): knowledge of the unseen. Fortune telling includes reading horoscopes.

Many Muslims today argue that they only listen to the fortune-teller or read their horoscope for fun, and they do not believe in either of them. However, this is similar to the person who watches acts of magic for fun. There is also a hadith stating a clear punishment for this.

The Prophet (ﷺ) said: « Whoever goes to a fortune-teller and asks him about something, his prayers will not be accepted for forty nights. » (Muslim)

The person still has to pray during these forty days but will get no reward for it, as a punishment for the sin. If he or she does not pray, that will be considered as a separate sin.

Finally, many Muslims today see nothing wrong with watching people indulging in acts of shirk in films. This is especially common in Bollywood[9] movies, wherein the characters worship idols and actors sometimes play the role of Hindu gods. Yet many Muslims watch and enjoy such films. It is forbidden to enjoy seeing anybody doing an act of shirk, because it is compulsory for Muslims to hate shirk and kufr and to work to remove them from society.

Fornication, adultery and whatever leads to it

Perhaps the most natural and common means of enjoyment for humans is that of sexual intercourse. Islam caters to this need but has set logical limits of modesty and chastity, and limited it to being between spouses. Islam condemns *zinâ* in the strongest terms. Zinâ is the act of sexual intercourse outside marriage and involves varying levels of sin. It includes fornication, adultery and homosexuality. Islam has forbidden it in all its forms, as well as anything that leads to it. Allah (ﷻ) has warned us in the Qur'an:

﴿ وَلَا تَقْرَبُواْ ٱلزِّنَىٰٓ إِنَّهُۥ كَانَ فَٰحِشَةً وَسَآءَ سَبِيلًا ۝ ﴾

(سورة بني إسرائيل: الآية ٣٢)

⟪And do not approach unlawful sexual intercourse. Indeed, it is ever an immorality and is evil as a way.⟫   *(Qur'an 17: 32)*

This verse prohibits entering all those doors that lead to zinâ. This includes lustful gazing at the opposite sex, unnecessary intermingling and being alone with a member of the opposite sex with whom zinâ is possible.

However, we find that the Western world has flung open its doors to sexual promiscuity. As a result, sexual entertainment has become the most famous form of entertainment, with the catch-phrase: "Sex sells!" Yet not too long ago, even in the West, modesty was upheld, and things that are regarded as entertainment today would have been frowned upon.

Dr. Abu Ameenah Bilal Philips has explained this drastic change in the following passage:

> During the fifties and sixties, a sexual revolution began in the West culminating in the removal of fornication and adultery from the law books as punishable crimes. When modern Western legislators analyzed fornication and marriage, they concluded that the only difference between the two was a piece of paper; the marriage certificate. It was only religious influence (The Ten Commandments) that had made fornication illegal. During that period lawmakers deduced a new principle to determine the legality of sexual relations between people.

Since rape was unanimously considered unacceptable, they concluded that the principle of "consent" must be present for such relations to be legally acceptable. They also all agreed that sexual relations between adults and children were wrong (paedophilia) since children could easily be taken advantage of by adults due to their immaturity. Consequently, they added the second principle of "adulthood" for legal sexual relations. The phrase "consenting adults" became the battle cry of the sexual revolution resulting in an upsurge or wife swapping parties, group sex, sadomasochism, topless bars, etc., among many elements of the society.[10]

All of the aforementioned forms of entertainment are strictly prohibited in Islam and should be regarded as filth. There are many reasons why Islam has prohibited these sins; they lead to loose morals which threaten the very fabric of family life. Disloyalty between spouses, incest, shame, confusion in lineage and the spread of sexually transmitted diseases (STDs) are only some of the many reasons such acts are evil and prohibited. Sexual promiscuity also goes against the goal of the Sharia to protect the progeny of humanity. This is because it leads to abortions and illegitimate children, among other evils.

Anyone who wishes to enjoy a sexual experience is most welcome to do so with a spouse, behind closed doors; nobody else needs to know what they do together. Islam has recommended the most balanced, modest and natural allowance.

This category also includes watching fashion shows or ogling at models on the catwalk. Any form of entertainment that involves looking lustfully at the opposite sex is strictly prohibited. May Allah (ﷻ) save us from this test of our times.

Gambling and that which leads to it

Gambling and all its forms have been prohibited in the Qur'an and declared as filth from the devil. Allah (ﷻ) has said:

﴿ يَـٰٓأَيُّهَا ٱلَّذِينَ ءَامَنُوٓاْ إِنَّمَا ٱلۡخَمۡرُ وَٱلۡمَيۡسِرُ وَٱلۡأَنصَابُ وَٱلۡأَزۡلَـٰمُ رِجۡسٌ مِّنۡ عَمَلِ ٱلشَّيۡطَـٰنِ فَٱجۡتَنِبُوهُ لَعَلَّكُمۡ تُفۡلِحُونَ ۞ ﴾   (سورة المائدة: الآية ٩٠)

❮O you who have believed, indeed, intoxicants, gambling, [sacrificing on] stone altars [to other than Allah], and divining arrows are but defilement from the work of Satan, so avoid it that you may be successful.❯   *(Qur'an 5: 90)*

Gambling is the wagering of money, or something else of material value, on an event with an uncertain outcome. The intent is to win more than you have put in. Gambling is prohibited because it involves taking a risk in which, most of the time, you lose your money; you seldom win. It is an oppressive method of taking other people's money; it is strictly prohibited just as Islam prohibits all forms of oppression. Gambling also goes against the principle of preserving the economy.

Modern forms of gambling that are common include insurance, playing the lottery and competitions in which the participants pay a fee, such as SMS competitions where people pay more than the general SMS rate. Apart from insurance, other forms of gambling are generally done for fun, and lots of people waste their time and money in casinos.

It should be noted that, as with other major sins, anything that leads to gambling is also forbidden. Thus, one is not allowed to visit a casino even if one is not going to gamble. This is because it is a place of vice, and the environment will influence a person to commit sins.

Similarly, all games that lead to gambling are makrooh according to some scholars, and ḥarâm according to others. However, all scholars agree that if played for money, the game becomes ḥarâm. This includes backgammon and card games. Games played with dice also fall into this category, since they are based on chance and not on skill.

The Prophet (ﷺ) said: « He who plays with dice [backgammon] has disobeyed Allah and His Apostle. » (Abu Dâwood, Bayhaqi, Ḥâkim, Ibn Mâjah and Mâlik)[11]

Ibn Qudâmah said in the chapter on games in *Al-Mughni*:

Every game which involves gambling is ḥarâm, no matter what game it is. It is the gambling which Allah has commanded us to avoid, and the one who does that on a regular basis, his testimony is to be rejected. That which is free of gambling is the game in which there is no payment by both sides or either side. Some of these games are ḥarâm, and some are permissible. That which is ḥarâm is games with dice. This is the view of Imam Abu Ḥaneefah and most of the companions of Imam Shâfi'i.[12]

Abu Is-hâq has said: "Some of our scholars maintain that it's just detested and not unlawful."[13] Also, in the book *At-Targheeb Wat-Tarheeb,*[14] al-Mundhiri has quoted the majority of scholars as ruling that this game is unlawful.

Intoxicants

Anything which intoxicates a person and alters the senses is prohibited. It is not permitted to take even a single sip, drop or puff of such a substance, for the narrations prohibiting it are clear. The Qur'anic verse 5: 90, which was quoted above, puts taking intoxicants in the same league as idol worship and fortune telling.

The Prophet (ﷺ) has defined intoxicants as follows: « Anything that clouds the senses is an intoxicant, and anything that intoxicates is prohibited. » (Muslim)

He also said: « Whatever intoxicates in large quantities is prohibited in small quantities. » (A reliable hadith recorded by Abu Dâwood and at-Tirmidhi)

This category includes drinking any alcoholic beverage, smoking any intoxicating drug, and anything else that intoxicates a person. Similarly, anything that leads to consuming intoxicants is prohibited. Thus, gatherings where alcohol is served are prohibited, as are restaurants where alcohol is served, even if the meat there is ḥalâl.

Regarding the reason for the prohibition of such substances, it is common knowledge that throughout history, intoxication has been a major cause of chaos, violence and even death. When intoxicated, people forget Allah (ﷻ), and there is no limit to the type of sin they can commit in such a state.

Dr. Bilal Philips has explained this reasoning in the following passage:

> God, through Divine Law, has prohibited intoxicants and gambling primarily because they cause human beings to forget God. The human mind and body easily become addicted to drugs and games of chance. Once addicted, humankind's desire to continually be stimulated by them, leads them into all forms of corruption and violence among themselves.[15]

Sinful speech

Perhaps the most common form of prohibited entertainment is sinful speech. Many people today do not think twice about what they are saying; they forget that every word they utter is being recorded and will have to be accounted for on the last day. Today, people search for topics to talk about. They want to converse, regardless of the topic. Thus, many sins of the tongue are committed in such circles. This attitude is the opposite of that required of a believer, which is described in the following hadith:

The Prophet (ﷺ) said: « Whoever believes in Allah and the last day should either speak what is good or remain silent. » (Bukhari)

There are many forms of sinful speech, the most common of which is gossip. Gossip can be of two types: backbiting, which means to talk negatively about a person who is absent, even if what is being discussed is true. The second type is slandering, which means lying while speaking negatively about others. This category includes suspicion without evidence, mockery and looking for faults in others. Allah (ﷺ) has prohibited all of the above in the following verse:

﴿ يَٰٓأَيُّهَا ٱلَّذِينَ ءَامَنُوا۟ ٱجْتَنِبُوا۟ كَثِيرًا مِّنَ ٱلظَّنِّ إِنَّ بَعْضَ ٱلظَّنِّ إِثْمٌ وَلَا تَجَسَّسُوا۟ وَلَا يَغْتَب بَّعْضُكُم بَعْضًا أَيُحِبُّ أَحَدُكُمْ أَن يَأْكُلَ لَحْمَ أَخِيهِ مَيْتًا فَكَرِهْتُمُوهُ وَٱتَّقُوا۟ ٱللَّهَ إِنَّ ٱللَّهَ تَوَّابٌ رَّحِيمٌ ۝ ﴾ (سورة حجرات: الآية ١٢)

❨O you who have believed, avoid much [negative] assumption. Indeed, some assumption is sin. And do not spy or backbite each other. Would one of you like to eat the flesh of his brother when dead? You would detest it. And fear Allah; indeed, Allah is Accepting of repentance and Merciful.❩ *(Qur'an 49: 12)*

These sins of the tongue, which people treat lightly, are actually the root causes of disunity among the Muslims. If we are constantly thinking negatively about, looking for faults in, and spreading rumours about our fellow Muslims, how can we ever expect our hearts to be united?

Excessive laughter

It is human nature to enjoy a good joke and laugh. Islam does not prohibit this; it does not expect us to be strict and serious all the time. It allows laughter and humour. On many occasions, it has been reported that the Prophet (ﷺ) laughed so much that his molars became visible, as in the following narration:

« When the Messenger of Allah (ﷺ) arrived after the expedition to Tabook or Khaybar [the narrator is not sure which], the wind raised an end of a curtain that was hung in front of 'Â'ishah's storeroom, revealing some dolls that belonged to her.

He asked: What is this?

She replied: My dolls.

Among them, he saw a horse with wings made of rags, and he asked: What is this I see among them?

She replied: A horse.

He asked: What is this that it has on it?

She replied: Two wings.

He asked: A horse with two wings?

She replied: Have you not heard that Solomon had horses with wings? She said: Thereupon, the Apostle of Allah (ﷺ) laughed so heartily that I could see his molar teeth. » (A reliable hadith recorded by Abu Dâwood)

However, there are limits. The Prophet (ﷺ) has forbidden us from joking too much because it deadens the heart.

He said: « Do not laugh too much, for excessive laughter kills the heart [spiritually]. » (Ibn Mâjah; a sound hadith according to al-Albâni)

He also said: « If you knew that which I know, you would laugh little and weep much. » (Bukhari)

Thus, moderation is required even in humour. It is also vital to understand that there is a time for laughter and humour, and a time for seriousness and sobriety. The reason for this prohibition is that excessive laughter makes people take life less seriously, and they begin to see humour in everything. It also makes them so accustomed to humour that they are unable to sit through any serious speech. Such people find lectures boring and do not attend anything beneficial simply because they do not find it funny. This is what is meant by excessive laughter killing the heart.

Consequently, the current norm of watching too many comedies and sitcoms is completely unacceptable. It is difficult to find a person who is accustomed to laughing all day who still takes Islam seriously. Muslims should realise that life is serious and that there are some things they cannot joke about; there is a time for laughter and a time for seriousness.

It should also be noted that jokes that mock or degrade any demographic group or individual are completely prohibited, as are fabricated stories that make people laugh, unless the audience knows that they are not true. Of course, the best jokes are the ones based on true, daily-life anecdotes. There is no harm in narrating such incidents to others to share a laugh.

Regarding mockery and degradation, Allah (ﷻ) has informed us:

﴿ يَٰٓأَيُّهَا ٱلَّذِينَ ءَامَنُوا۟ لَا يَسْخَرْ قَوْمٌ مِّن قَوْمٍ عَسَىٰٓ أَن يَكُونُوا۟ خَيْرًا مِّنْهُمْ وَلَا نِسَآءٌ مِّن نِّسَآءٍ عَسَىٰٓ أَن يَكُنَّ خَيْرًا مِّنْهُنَّ ۖ وَلَا تَلْمِزُوٓا۟ أَنفُسَكُمْ وَلَا تَنَابَزُوا۟ بِٱلْأَلْقَٰبِ ۖ بِئْسَ ٱلِٱسْمُ ٱلْفُسُوقُ بَعْدَ ٱلْإِيمَٰنِ ۚ وَمَن لَّمْ يَتُبْ فَأُو۟لَٰٓئِكَ هُمُ ٱلظَّٰلِمُونَ ۝ ﴾

(سورة حجرات: الآية ١١)

﴾O you who have believed, let not a people ridicule [another] people; perhaps they may be better than them; nor let women ridicule [other] women; perhaps they may be better than them. And do not insult one another and do not call each other by [offensive] nicknames. Wretched is the name [that is, mention] of disobedience after [one's] faith. And whoever does not repent – then it is those who are the wrongdoers.﴿ *(Qur'an 49: 11)*

As for lying when making jokes, the Prophet (ﷺ) said: « Woe to him who lies to make people laugh. Woe to him! Woe to him! » (A reliable hadith recorded by Abu Dâwood)

Finally, the worst type of joke is one about Allah (ﷻ), His messenger or anything related to Islam. Such jokes take a person out of the fold of Islam and are regarded as kufr. The following incident, quoted in *Tafsir ibn Kathir*, and the verses revealed during it, prove this point:

> In the course of the campaign of Tabuk, a man came up one day and declared, "We have seen no people with greater appetite, more lying, or more cowardly in battle than the Prophet of Allah (ﷺ) and his reciting companions." 'Awf ibn Mâlik rose and said, "It is rather you that are the liar. You are a hypocrite, pretending to be a Muslim. I shall tell the Prophet of Allah (ﷺ) about you." 'Awf then went to the Prophet (ﷺ) to inform him, but found that revelation had already preceded him. [When the news reached] the man, he mounted on his camel, sought the Prophet of Allah (ﷺ) and said, "But we were only joking, trying to pass the time while traveling." Ibn 'Umar (ﷺ) said, "He was clinging to the saddle belt of the Prophet's camel as it ran, his feet and legs being battered by the rough ground, and repeating, 'But we were only joking,' and the Prophet (ﷺ) insisting without turning his face to him: 'Joking? Joking with Allah (ﷻ)? With His revelation? With His Prophet?'"[16]

Consequently, certain practices that are rife among some Muslims – such as mocking the *ḥijâb* (veil ordained by Allah for believing women), the beard or polygamy, among other things – amount to an extremely unacceptable sin and are considered equal to kufr. It is a sign of hypocrisy; a person claims verbally to be a Muslim, but inwardly hates Islam or certain aspects of it.

Musical instruments and immoral songs

This particular issue deserves a lengthy explanation since it has become a topic that is often debated in the Muslim community today. It is important, however, to take an unbiased look at the various views on this issue and accept that there is a difference of opinion regarding the prohibition of musical instruments. I say this because many of the scholars who hold the view that music is prohibited claim that there is a consensus on this issue, which is not true.

﴿ وَمِنَ ٱلنَّاسِ مَن يَشْتَرِى لَهْوَ ٱلْحَدِيثِ لِيُضِلَّ عَن سَبِيلِ ٱللَّهِ بِغَيْرِ عِلْمٍ وَيَتَّخِذَهَا هُزُوًا ۚ أُوْلَٰٓئِكَ لَهُمْ عَذَابٌ مُّهِينٌ ۝ ﴾ (سورة لقمان: الآية ٦)

⟨And of the people is he who buys the amusement of speech to mislead [others] from the way of Allah without knowledge and who takes it [meaning His way] in ridicule. Those will have a humiliating punishment.⟩ *(Qur'an 31: 6)*

This verse has been explained by the Companions (may Allah be pleased with them) and succeeding scholars to refer, firstly, to immoral songs and, secondly, to any idle speech which distracts people from the straight path.

An issue which is hotly debated today is the permissibility of using musical instruments. It is generally accepted that most of the music produced by the disbelievers today is ḥarâm because of its inappropriate content and messages. However, the Muslims are divided over the use of musical instruments when accompanied by permissible lyrics. This difference is based mainly on two hadiths in *Ṣaḥeeḥ al-Bukhâri* that seem to contradict each other. The first of these is the previously mentioned hadith of the young girls playing with the hand-drum (duff) and the Prophet (ﷺ) approving it. In fact, there are many hadiths in which he allowed the playing of the hand-drum.

In the second hadith, the Prophet (ﷺ) prophesised: « From among my followers, there will be some people who will consider illegal sexual intercourse, the wearing of silk [for men], the drinking of alcoholic drinks and the use of musical instruments as lawful. » (Bukhari)

This hadith is clear in its wording that musical instruments are prohibited and are considered to be in the same category as alcohol and adultery. It should be noted that its chain of narrators, as mentioned in *Saheeh al-Bukhâri,* is broken. However, this hadith has been quoted in a number of other hadith compilations, with other chains of narrators, and it is definitely authentic.

Scholars have generally taken the position that this hadith mentions the general ruling on musical instruments, while the preceding hadith mentions the exception. Yet they differ as to what extent this exception covers. Some say it refers only to the hand-drum, which can only be played by women and children, others restrict it to the days of celebration and prohibit it on other days, and yet others allow it in general. They also differ over whether the exception applies only to the hand-drum or whether other forms of drums and percussion instruments are included.

This is as far as the exception is stretched by the majority of scholars; however, other scholars, like Ibn Ḥazm and Imam al-Ghazâli, held that musical instruments are permissible. In their view, the content and effect of the songs, and what they lead to, determines whether they are permissible or forbidden. They interpreted the above hadith as referring to music that accompanies fornication or drinking of alcohol; they also argued that every authentic hadith that prohibits music does so along with prohibiting fornication and alcohol.

Imam al-Ghazâli wrote a lengthy treatise on this topic, in which he explained his view and stated his evidence. This treatise can be found in his *Ihyâ' 'Uloom ad-Deen,* which has been translated into English. After a lengthy discussion of the various opinions and evidence regarding this issue, Imam al-Ghazâli concluded that he believed the prohibition of music is not general but is limited to certain situations. If music leads to drinking alcohol, fornication and other such vices, then it is prohibited. Yet if it brings people closer to Allah Almighty (ﷻ), it can be regarded as permissible. He mentioned other conditions, all of which can be found in his *Ihyâ' 'Uloom ad-Deen* in the chapter on music.

Imam Shawkâni wrote an important book on this issue titled *Ibtâl Da'watul Ijmâ' 'alâ Tahreem Mutlaqis Simâ* (Refuting the Claim of Consensus on the General Prohibition of Music), in which he listed various views and proofs that scholars have on this issue. Bear in mind that Imam Shawkâni was of the opinion that musical instruments are prohibited, but he wrote this book to ensure that people did not go to extremes in dealing with those who consider music permissible. Imam Shawkâni said at the end of this book:

> There is no doubt, after all the views and proofs that we have mentioned, that music is among the doubtful issues, and believers should be wary regarding the doubtful issues. It is narrated in *Saheeh al-Bukhâri*: "Whoever leaves the doubtful issues has protected his honour and his religion."[17]

Imam Shawkâni also states:

> Allah knows that we do not sit at the gatherings of music… but we mentioned this from the point of view of evidence… so that it becomes clear that this is not an issue where one can claim that the followers of a certain opinion are misguided. Rather, how can those who claim that there is no difference of opinion regarding the issue of music be guided to the path of justice?[18]

Taking all of the above into consideration, the safest opinion is to follow the majority of scholars and abstain from music which involves stringed and wind instruments. At the same time, one should remember that there is a difference of opinion on this issue, so it would not be fair to label those who sincerely believe in the permissibility of musical instruments as deviant or as disbelievers. On the contrary, they are our Muslim brothers and sisters who are following a minority opinion, and Allah Almighty (ﷻ) knows best which opinion is correct.

It should be noted, though, that when individuals hear music but are not paying attention to it, they are not sinning. This is similar to those who are not rewarded if they hear the Qur'an but do not pay attention to it. This is an important point to note since it sometimes becomes difficult to avoid music altogether – such as in shopping centres and other areas. Shaykh al-Islam, Ibn Taymiyah, has said:

> The command and the prohibition have to do with listening. Merely hearing something is like seeing; it has to do with the intention behind seeing, not what happens without a person choosing it… The same applies to committing sin through the five senses of hearing, sight, smell, taste and touch; the commands and prohibitions are connected to what a person intends and does, but whatever happens without him choosing it, there is no command or prohibition with regard to that.[19]

Celebrating the festivals of the disbelievers

Allah (ﷻ) Almighty has given us two holy days for celebration, worship and fun. These are the days of *Eid al-Aḍḥâ* (at the culmination of the hajj) and *Eid al-Fiṭr* (at the end of the fasting month of Ramadan).

« Anas ibn Mâlik (ﷺ) narrated: The Prophet (ﷺ) came to Madinah during two days in which they played. The Prophet (ﷺ) asked: What are these two days? They said: These are two days we used to play in, during the time of ignorance. The Prophet (ﷺ) said: Allah has

replaced them with two better days: Eid al-Aḍḥâ and Eid al- Fiṭr. »
(A sound hadith recorded by Abu Dâwood, Aḥmad and Ibn Ḥajar
al-'Asqalâni)

It is clear that the Prophet (ﷺ) did not allow them to continue
their play and celebration because it was a custom of the pagan
Arabs of Madinah. Instead, he told them: « Allah has replaced
them », meaning that you must leave what was replaced and go with
that which replaced them.

From the above narration, we can easily see that the
Prophet (ﷺ) did not allow his Companions to celebrate and play on
these days since it was part of another religion. This ruling extends to
the celebration of all holidays with religious backgrounds, including
Christmas, Diwali, Easter and Halloween. It is not permissible to
join in the celebration of any such holiday, even if it has lost its
religious significance. This is because its roots are in shirk, and as
Muslims, we cannot glorify shirk.

This prohibition extends to the celebration of birthdays, since
that is an ancient pagan custom with its roots in Greek mythology.
It also falls into the category of celebrations of ignorance.

'Umar ibn al-Khaṭṭâb (ﷺ) said: "Keep away from the enemies
of Allah on their holidays."[20]

Similarly, such innovated celebrations as *mawlid* (the
Prophet's birthday) and *'urs* (the anniversary of someone's death)
are also prohibited. This is not because they are celebrations, but
because they are religious innovations with no basis in the Qur'an,
the Sunnah, or the teachings of the early righteous generations.

Contrary to the belief of some Muslims, it is permissible and
encouraged to celebrate and to enjoy permissible forms of fun on
the days of Eid. Some Muslims claim that we should spend these
days in worship only, but the Sunnah proves otherwise. First of all,
fasting on the days of Eid is prohibited. If these days were intended

for worship only, then why would this great form of worship be prohibited? Secondly, the word 'Eid' itself means a happy occasion or a holiday.

A major proof that it is permissible to have fun on the days of Eid is the following famous hadith, which was mentioned previously:

« It has been narrated by 'Â'ishah (🌸), the wife of the Prophet, that once the Prophet Muhammad (🕌) came home, and at that time, two little girls were singing songs about the battle of Bu'âth. The Prophet (🕌) lay down on the bed and turned his face away. Then Abu Bakr (🌸) came and scolded her, saying: These musical instruments of Satan in the house of the Prophet of Allah (🕌)! Prophet Muhammad turned to him and said: Leave them. In the words of 'Â'ishah (🌸): When Abu Bakr got busy in other matters, I told the two girls to leave, and they left. That was the day of Eid. The Abyssinians were playing in the mosque with shields and lances. Then either I asked the Messenger (🕌), or he himself said: Do you want to have a look? I said yes, so he let me stand behind him, with my cheek against his cheek, and said: Carry on, Banu Arfidah. When I became bored, he asked: Is that enough for you? I said yes. He said: Then you may leave. » (Bukhari)

That is the ruling regarding religious celebrations. As for other celebrations that are not of a religious nature – such as celebrating a special achievement like a child memorising the Qur'an or getting good grades at school – these are permissible as long as they do not include anything harâm. It is known that the Prophet (🕌) encouraged the celebration of marriage with a wedding banquet hosted by the groom. Allah Almighty (🕌) knows best.

Chess and other games

There are different views on playing chess. Many scholars – including Imam Abu Haneefah, Imam Shâfi'i and Ibn Qayyim – said that chess is ḥarâm. Imam Mâlik was of the view that it is makrooh. Yaḥyâ said that he heard Mâlik say: There is no good in chess, and he disapproved of it. Yaḥyâ said: I heard him disapprove of playing it and other worthless games.[21]

In his well-known book, *The Lawful and the Prohibited in Islam*, Shaykh Yusuf al-Qaradâwi explains that the Prophet's Companions (may Allah be pleased with them all) also had different opinions:

> Ibn 'Umar said that it is worse than backgammon and 'Ali regarded it as gambling (perhaps meaning when it is played for money), while some others merely expressed disapproval of it.

> However, some Companions and some of the second generation scholars allowed it. Among these were Ibn 'Abbas, Abu Hurairah, Ibn Sirin, Hisham bin 'Umrah and Sa'id bin al-Musayyib. We agree with those great jurists, since the original principle is the permissibility of acts and no text is to be found prohibiting it.

An analysis of the hadiths used as proof for prohibiting chess shows that they are not authentic. Because of this, scholars like Ibn Ḥazm have taken the stance that chess is not prohibited, especially since there are benefits in playing this game. Shaykh al-Qaradâwi mentions that chess:

> Is also a mental exercise which requires thought and planning. In this respect it is the opposite of backgammon, for while backgammon is a game of chance and therefore comparable to divining with arrows, chess is a game of skill and strategy, which may be compared to archery.

Of course, playing chess would be considered ḥarâm if it involved gambling or any of the items listed below under 'General prohibitions'.

It should also be noted that the following is a mistranslation: « He who played chess is like one who dyed his hand with the flesh and blood of swine. » (Muslim)

The word mentioned in this hadith is *nard*, which means backgammon; the Arabic word for chess is *shatranj*. A more authentic translation is: « He who plays with dice will be deemed as a person thrusting his hands in pig's blood. » (Muslim)

Games that are played with dice are generally ruled to be makrooh because they involve an element of chance. They are regarded as ḥarâm if played as a means of gambling, because of this hadith, which was explained in detail in the chapter on gambling:

The Prophet (ﷺ) said: « He who plays with dice has disobeyed Allah and His Apostle. » (Abu Dâwood, Bayhaqi, Ḥâkim, Ibn Mâjah and Mâlik)[22]

General prohibitions

Aside from the categories we have mentioned, all other forms of entertainment are permissible if they meet the following conditions:

1. It should not distract us from our obligations, religious or worldly, as Allah (ﷻ) has said in the Qur'an:

﴿ وَمِنَ ٱلنَّاسِ مَن يَشۡتَرِي لَهۡوَ ٱلۡحَدِيثِ لِيُضِلَّ عَن سَبِيلِ ٱللَّهِ بِغَيۡرِ عِلۡمٍ وَيَتَّخِذَهَا هُزُوًا أُوْلَـٰٓئِكَ لَهُمۡ عَذَابٌ مُّهِينٌ ۝ ﴾

(سورة لقمان: الآية ٦)

﴾And of the people is he who buys the amusement of speech to mislead [others] from the way of Allah without knowledge and who takes it [that is, His way] in ridicule. Those will have a humiliating punishment.﴿

(Qur'an 31: 6)

Thus, any idle pastime which distracts people from their duties is prohibited.

2. It should not lead to any of the aforementioned sins. It should not contain even the slightest elements of them. An example of this is a video game in which one has to commit a sin; such a game would be ḥarâm.

3. We must avoid extravagance and wasting of time and money, for we are accountable to Allah (ﷻ) for every cent and second we spend. We must observe moderation. Allah (ﷻ) has said:

﴿ ... وَلَا تُبَذِّرْ تَبْذِيرًا ۝ إِنَّ ٱلْمُبَذِّرِينَ كَانُوٓاْ إِخْوَٰنَ ٱلشَّيَٰطِينِ وَكَانَ ٱلشَّيْطَٰنُ لِرَبِّهِۦ كَفُورًا ۝ ﴾ (سورة بني إسرائيل: الآية ٢٦ – ٢٧)

﴿...do not spend wastefully. Indeed, the wasteful are brothers of the devils, and ever has Satan been to his Lord ungrateful.﴾ *(Qur'an 17: 26-27)*

4. We should not allow ourselves to become addicted to any form of entertainment, as this will eventually lead to indulgence and negligence of the more important things in life. The following verse of the Qur'an would apply to such a person:

﴿ ٱلَّذِينَ ٱتَّخَذُواْ دِينَهُمْ لَهْوًا وَلَعِبًا وَغَرَّتْهُمُ ٱلْحَيَوٰةُ ٱلدُّنْيَا فَٱلْيَوْمَ نَنسَىٰهُمْ كَمَا نَسُواْ لِقَآءَ يَوْمِهِمْ هَٰذَا وَمَا كَانُواْ بِـَٔايَٰتِنَا يَجْحَدُونَ ۝ ﴾ (سورة أعراف: الآية ٥١)

﴿Who took their religion as distraction and amusement and whom the worldly life deluded. So today We will forget them just as they forgot the meeting of this day of theirs and for having rejected Our verses.❭   *(Qur'an 7: 51)*

If the above limits are adhered to, then *inshallah* (God willing), we will be able to save ourselves and enjoy all that which Allah (ﷻ) has permitted, with a clear conscience.

Chapter Five

Recommended forms of entertainment

$\mathcal{I}$f the aforementioned limits are adhered to, all other forms of entertainment would be considered ḥalâl. There are, however, some forms of entertainment that have been encouraged in Islam by the Prophet (ﷺ). We should strive to use these means to entertain ourselves.

Spending time with spouse and children

There is no form of relaxation and fun more rewarding in both the worlds than that of spending time with one's family. The Prophet's encouragement of this can be found in many hadiths mentioning that he played, joked and raced with his wives. They would tell him stories, and he would play with the children and make them laugh. The Prophet (ﷺ) was a role model as a family man. Indeed, it would take an entire book to discuss the Prophet (ﷺ) as a role model within the family.

Spending time with one's family and having fun together is a major factor in keeping the family united and close. It develops trust and love for each other and brings peace to the household. True Muslims find peace and enjoyment at home with their own families and do not need to escape from them to be entertained. It is this family unity that has been lost in the modern age, when each member of the family lives a separate life. Sadly, although the members of a family may live under one roof, they may not even meet to share a meal together. If we are to revive the unity of our families, we must revive the concept of family time.

The following are some hadiths that shed light on the importance of and reward for spending time with one's family:

The Prophet (ﷺ) said: « Any act devoid of the remembrance of Allah is void except four: shooting, training a horse, playing with one's family and swimming. » (Recorded by Bayhaqi and aṭ-Ṭabarâni with a good chain of narrators)

« 'Â'ishah (ﵞ) narrated that while she was on a journey with the Messenger of Allah, she had a race with the Prophet (ﷺ) and won. Later, after she had gained some weight, she again had a race with him, and he won. He said: This is for that. » (A sound hadith recorded by Abu Dâwood)

The Prophet (ﷺ) said: « When a Muslim spends something on his family, intending to receive Allah's reward, it is regarded as charity for him. » (Bukhari)

The time that married couples spend together also falls into this category. Besides spending time with the children, it is important that spouses spend time with each other, enjoying each other's company and increasing their love for each other. Sex, including foreplay, is an important ingredient for a happy married life; it is also an act for which one is rewarded. One of the best forms of permissible entertainment is for spouses to enjoy each other physically. The only specific prohibitions between a husband and wife are anal sex and sex during a woman's menstrual period and post-natal period. Anything else that spouses do to satisfy each other is permissible, but it is forbidden for the husband or the wife to discuss their sexual relations with others. The following are some important hadiths regarding spousal relationships:

The Prophet (ﷺ) said: « You shall be rewarded for every deed that you perform solely for Allah's pleasure, even if that deed is putting something in the mouth of your wife. » (Bukhari)

The Prophet (ﷺ) once told a young Companion who married an older, previously-married woman: « Why haven't you married a virgin who would have played with you, and you would have played with her? » (Bukhari)

The Prophet (ﷺ) said: « Every *tasbeeh* [saying *subhân Allâh* (glory be to Allah)] is charity; every *takbeer* [saying *Allâhu Akbar* (Allah is the Greatest)] is charity, every *tamheed* [saying *alhamdulillâh* (all praise is for Allah)] is charity, every *tahleel* [saying *lâ ilâha illâ Allâh* (there is no God but Allah)] is charity, enjoining what is good is charity, forbidding what is evil is charity and in your sexual act is charity. The Companions asked: Oh Messenger of Allah! How can one of us get rewarded for fulfilling his desires? The Prophet (ﷺ) replied: Do you not see that you are sinning and are punished if you fulfil it in a harâm manner? Similarly, you get rewarded for fulfilling it in a halâl manner. » (Muslim)

Pondering the creation of Allah (ﷺ)

In many places in the Qur'an, Allah (ﷺ) has invited us to ponder and reflect on His beautiful creation as a means of getting to know Him; increasing our love, awe and respect for Him; and increasing our faith. Pondering the creation of Allah (ﷺ) is also one of the best ways of relaxing the mind. One truly finds peace in one's heart when surrounded by nature.

Different recreational methods of pondering over Allah's creation include visiting nature reserves and other places where animals are present, watching nature documentaries and taking walks on the beach or in the park. All of these are recommended ways of enjoying Allah's creation.

﴿ إِنَّ فِى خَلْقِ ٱلسَّمَـٰوَٰتِ وَٱلْأَرْضِ وَٱخْتِلَـٰفِ ٱلَّيْلِ وَٱلنَّهَارِ لَآيَـٰتٍ لِّأُوْلِى ٱلْأَلْبَـٰبِ ۝ ٱلَّذِينَ يَذْكُرُونَ ٱللَّهَ قِيَـٰمًا وَقُعُودًا وَعَلَىٰ جُنُوبِهِمْ وَيَتَفَكَّرُونَ فِى خَلْقِ ٱلسَّمَـٰوَٰتِ وَٱلْأَرْضِ رَبَّنَا مَا خَلَقْتَ هَـٰذَا بَـٰطِلًا سُبْحَـٰنَكَ فَقِنَا عَذَابَ ٱلنَّارِ ۝ ﴾

(سورة آل عمران: الآية ١٩٠ — ١٩١)

﴿Indeed, in the creation of the heavens and the earth and the alternation of the night and the day are signs for those of understanding – who remember Allah while standing or sitting or [lying] on their sides and give thought to the creation of the heavens and the earth [saying]: Our Lord, You did not create this aimlessly; exalted are You [above such a thing]; then protect us from the punishment of the fire.﴾

(Qur'an 3: 190-191)

Physical activities

Participating in a physical sport is a recommended form of entertainment. The specific forms of sports that the Prophet (ﷺ) recommended – or participated in himself – include foot races, horse races, wrestling (or any form of self-defence training), swimming and archery.

Physical sports are important to keep Muslims fit and ready to defend themselves, their families or their religion, should the need ever arise. Islam places great emphasis on maintaining the body, but one should note that moderation is important.

While Islam prohibits us from overeating, being lazy and growing fat as a result of it, it is not right for Muslims who excel at sports to force others to be like they are. Allah (ﷻ) has created humans with different interests. Some may be interested in sports, while others may prefer books and studying, and there may be some exceptional ones who do both. All of this is acceptable as long as people take decent care of their bodies and do not become unfit; this is the minimum that Muslims should do. More than this is recommended, of course, but a sport should not be forced on a person who is not interested in it.

This is an important point for Muslim parents to note, because it is important to take into consideration the personality and interests of each child and channel them in an appropriate direction. It can be very harmful to the children's mindset and relationship with you if you force them into things that they are not interested in.

The following hadiths prove that physical sports are recommended:

The Prophet (صلى الله عليه وسلم) said: « Any act of entertainment done by a believer is void (*bâṭil*) except three: playing with one's family, training a horse and practicing shooting. » (A reliable hadith recorded by Aḥmad and at-Tirmidhi) A detailed explanation of this hadith has been given in Chapter Three.

« 'Â'ishah (رضى الله عنها) narrated that while she was on a journey with the Messenger of Allah, she had a race with him (صلى الله عليه وسلم) and won. Later, after she had gained some weight, she again had a race with him, and he won. He said: This is for that. » (A sound hadith recorded by Abu Dâwood)

« The Prophet (صلى الله عليه وسلم) passed by some people of the tribe of Bani Aslam who were practicing archery. He said: O Bani Ismâ'eel! Practice archery, as your father Ismâ'eel was a great archer. Keep on throwing arrows, and I am with Bani so-and-so. One of the parties ceased throwing. Allah's Apostle asked: Why do you not throw? They replied: How can we throw while you are with them [that is, on their side]? Hearing that, the Prophet (صلى الله عليه وسلم) said: Throw, and I am with all of you. » (Bukhari)

The Prophet (صلى الله عليه وسلم) said: « Whoever learns archery and then gives it up is not from us. » (Muslim)

However, the ruling for watching professional sports is different, although playing sports or watching others perform them is permissible as proven by the following hadith:

'Â'ishah (☺) narrated: « I recall that once the Messenger of Allah (☺) screened me with his mantle, and I saw the sports of the Abyssinians. I was only a girl, and so you can well imagine how a girl of tender age is fond of watching the sport. » (Muslim)

Thus, watching a sport is permissible in itself, as long as there is nothing wrong with the content; for example, the participants of a sport should not be dressed in a ḥarâm manner.

Despite this, though, I strongly discourage watching professional sports competitions for the following reasons:

1. Wasting time: There is no doubt that fans of any professional sport waste many hours of their lives watching every match they can. This leads to their neglecting their duties to Allah (☺) and to other people. Such people often choose to watch a match over attending an Islamic programme, which is not the attitude of a believer.

2. Wasting knowledge: Sports fans tend to know the names and life stories of many players of their favourite teams, yet because of their preoccupation with this useless information – which will not even benefit them **in this world,** let alone the hereafter – such people tend to be ignorant of Islamic knowledge. This is completely unacceptable and ḥarâm.

3. Hero worship: Some fans of professional sports begin to exaggerate in praising their favourite players, and they try to emulate and revere them in every way. This leads to hero worship, including having more reverence for the sports player (generally a disbeliever) than the heroes of Islam and even the Prophet (☺), and many sins are committed

because of this. Such people would prefer to imitate their favourite sports players rather than the Prophet (ﷺ), which is a great act of disrespect and could reach the levels of kufr. Ibn al-Qayyim said:

> One day Shaykh al-Islam Ibn Taymiyah (may Allah sanctify his soul) said to me concerning some permissible matter, 'This does not befit a man who aspires to attain a high status, even though avoiding it is not a condition of salvation. The wise man will refrain from many permissible things so as to protect himself, especially if that permissible thing falls in between ḥalâl and ḥarâm.'[23]

For these reasons, among others, I strongly discourage Muslims from following professional sports. If one wishes to watch a sport, it should be a casual viewing, and the players should be Muslims. This is to ensure that one avoids seeing anything that is ḥarâm. We should organise our own sports tournaments, in which some youth can participate and others can watch. This way, none of the limits of the Sharia will be broken.

Beneficial books, stories, games and videos

Anything that benefits Muslims and brings them closer to Allah (ﷻ), or benefits them in an aspect of science, is recommended in Islam, as long as it is free from prohibited content. The Qur'an is full of stories that have many lessons. Allah (ﷻ) has informed us:

$$ \text{﴿ لَقَدۡ كَانَ فِى قَصَصِهِمۡ عِبۡرَةٌ لِّأُوْلِى ٱلۡأَلۡبَٰبِ ... ﴾} $$

(سورة يوسف: الآية ١١١)

❝There was certainly in their stories a lesson for those of understanding...❞ *(Qur'an 12: 111)*

From this verse, we come to understand that the stories of Islam should to be analysed for their lessons and not just learned for historical value. We can further deduce from this verse that any story from which a person can benefit is recommended.

Of course, priority should be given to the stories of the Qur'an and the life of the Prophet (ﷺ), as well as his Companions (may Allah be pleased with them) and the pious predecessors. However, as long as a story contains morals and lessons, we can read or listen to it and learn from it.

The same ruling applies more broadly to include any other form of media. If a game is beneficial, it should be given preference over those that just waste time. If a video is beneficial, it should be given preference over other ḥalāl videos. In any area of entertainment, one should seek out and give preference to the beneficial over the futile, even if the latter is permissible.

﴿ ... فَٱقْصُصِ ٱلْقَصَصَ لَعَلَّهُمْ يَتَفَكَّرُونَ ۝ ﴾   (سورة أعراف: الآية ١٧٦)

﴿...So relate the stories that perhaps they will give thought.﴾
(Qur'an 7: 176)

In general, any game, video or story that is not beneficial and does not waste time would be permissible in itself, although it is recommended to choose that which is beneficial over it.

﴿ وَمِنَ ٱلنَّاسِ مَن يَشْتَرِى لَهْوَ ٱلْحَدِيثِ لِيُضِلَّ عَن سَبِيلِ ٱللَّهِ بِغَيْرِ عِلْمٍ وَيَتَّخِذَهَا هُزُوًا أُوْلَٰٓئِكَ لَهُمْ عَذَابٌ مُّهِينٌ ۝ ﴾   (سورة لقمان: الآية ٦)

﴿And of the people is he who buys the amusement of speech to mislead [others] from the way of Allah without knowledge and who takes it [meaning His way] in ridicule. Those will have a humiliating punishment.﴾   *(Qur'an 31: 6)*

This verse has been explained by the Companions (may Allah be pleased with them) and later scholars to refer firstly to musical instruments and idle songs, and secondly to any idle speech that distracts people from the straight path.

Nasheeds (Islamic songs)

The music industry has gained so much popularity that an Islamic alternative is greatly needed. In fact, to face the current situation, it is recommended that Muslims produce and promote wholesome Islamic songs that spread the teachings and morals of Islam. Songs have a strong influence on people. Thus, we should be choosing songs that influence us to be better Muslims rather than listening to the evil that is promoted through popular modern songs.

Alḥamdulillâh, today we find the nasheed industry on the rise. Unfortunately, however, many singers are using musical instruments. We should try our best to stay away from nasheeds with music and stick to those that are definitely permissible. Children who are raised with nasheeds should be encouraged from an early age to be practising Muslims.

Proofs for the permissibility of nasheeds and the hand-drum include the following:

« It has been narrated by 'Â'ishah (🌸), the wife of the Prophet, that once the Prophet Muhammad (ﷺ) came home, and at that time, two little girls were singing songs about the battle of Bu'âth. The Prophet (ﷺ) lay down on the bed and turned his face away. Then Abu Bakr (؉) came and scolded her, saying: These musical instruments of Satan in the house of the Prophet of Allah (ﷺ)! Prophet Muhammad turned to him and said: Leave them. In the words of 'Â'ishah (🌸): When Abu Bakr got busy in other matters, I told the two girls to leave, and they left. That was the day of Eid. The Abyssinians were playing in the mosque with shields and lances. Then either I asked the Messenger (ﷺ), or he himself said: Do you want to have a look? I said yes, so he let me stand behind him, with my cheek against his cheek, and said: Carry on, Banu Arfidah. When I became bored, he asked: Is that enough for you? I said yes. He said: Then you may leave. » (Bukhari)

« 'Â'ishah (🌸) narrated that on the days of Mina (the 11ᵗʰ, 12ᵗʰ, and 13ᵗʰ days of the Islamic month of Dhul-Ḥijjah), Abu Bakr (🌸) came to her while two young girls were beating the duff [hand-drum] and the Prophet (🌸) was lying covered with his clothes. Abu Bakr scolded them, and the Prophet (🌸) uncovered his face and said to Abu Bakr: Leave them, for these days are the days of Eid and the days of Mina. » (Bukhari)

« Ar-Rabi bint Mu'awwidh narrated: After the consummation of my marriage, the Prophet (🌸) came and sat on my bed as far from me as you are sitting now. Our little girls started beating the tambourines and reciting lamenting verses, mourning my father who had been killed in the battle of Badr. One of them said: Among us is a Prophet who knows what will happen tomorrow. Hearing that, the Prophet (🌸) said: Leave this [saying] and keep on saying the verses that you had been saying before. » (Bukhari)

Dolls and toys that represent living things

Many scholars hold the view that dolls of living beings are prohibited as toys because of the general prohibition of drawing and sculpting animate objects, as narrated by 'Â'ishah (🌸) in the following hadith:

« I bought a cushion that had pictures [of animals]. When Allah's Apostle (🌸) saw it, he stood at the door and did not enter. I noticed the sign of disapproval on his face and said: O Allah's Apostle! I repent to Allah and His Apostle. What sin have I committed? Allah's Apostle asked: What is this cushion? I replied: I have bought it for you so that you may sit on it and recline on it. Allah's Apostle said: The makers of these pictures will be punished on the Day of Resurrection. It will be said to them: Give life to what you have created [that is, these pictures]. The Prophet (🌸) added: The angels [of mercy] do not enter a house in which there are pictures [of animals]. » (Bukhari)

However, children's toys are an exception to this ruling, as proven by the following hadith, also narrated by 'Â'ishah (🌸):

« I used to play with dolls in the presence of the Prophet (🌸), and my girlfriends also used to play with me. When Allah's Apostle used to enter [my dwelling place], they used to hide themselves. However, the Prophet would call them to join and play with me. » (Bukhari)

« When the Messenger of Allah (🌸) arrived after the expedition to Tabook or Khaybar [the narrator is not sure which], the wind raised an end of a curtain that was hung in front of 'Â'ishah's storeroom, revealing some dolls which belonged to her.

He asked: What is this?

She replied: My dolls.

Among them, he saw a horse with wings made of rags, and he asked: What is this I see among them?

She replied: A horse.

He asked: What is this that it has on it?

She replied: Two wings.

He asked: A horse with two wings?

She replied: Have you not heard that Solomon had horses with wings? She said: Thereupon, the Apostle of Allah (🌸) laughed so heartily that I could see his molar teeth. » (A reliable hadith recorded by Abu Dâwood)

Narrated 'Â'ishah (🌸): « Allah's messenger married me when I was seven years old. I was taken to his house as a bride when I was nine, and my dolls were with me. » When he died, she was eighteen years old. (Muslim)

A Companion, Ar-Rabi bint Mu'awwidh (👒), said:

We used to fast on that day [*'Âshoorah*²⁴] and also make the children fast. We would make toy figures out of wool for them, and if any of them cried for food, he would be given one until it was time to break the fast.²⁵

This exception can be extended to include all forms of animation intended for children as long as the content is not harâm. Some scholars also include all forms of animation with an educational benefit, which would include children's books with pictures and animated videos with halâl content.

In this regard, Shaykh Nâṣiruddin al-Albâni stated:

These two hadiths (the hadith of 'Â'ishah's dolls and the hadith about the Companions' practice of giving their fasting children toy figures to distract them from their hunger) indicate the permissibility of creating images and of owning them when there is an educational benefit in doing so, one that will help in the cultivation and development of the personality. Whatever else is of benefit to the Muslims and Islam may be included in the same ruling of permissibility of picture making and use, but everything besides that remains under the basic prohibition.²⁶

Providing alternatives

The final point I would like to mention on this topic is that it is recommended that Muslim parents, scholars and community leaders provide permissible alternatives to our children and youth to replace all that the West has produced. Cinemas, nightclubs and other dens of vice are extremely alluring and attractive, while many Muslims have made their homes and mosques hostile to the youth. In such a situation, we should not be surprised when the youth fall into sin to entertain themselves.

It is important that we establish alternatives to entertain our youth while benefiting them and helping them grow as Muslims. Ḥalâl entertainment centres, nasheeds, Islamic videos and games should be developed for the benefit and protection of the Muslim community. We should invest great effort in producing high quality Islamic products and attractive Islamic entertainment centres to draw the youth away from the traps of Satan.

These ideas may seem novel to many Muslims, and some may reject them, but we need to think realistically. These challenges and forms of entertainment did not exist in the past, so there was no need to develop alternatives. However, our current social context demands that we take action and develop practical solutions to the problem of Western entertainment. People should also remember the principle that everything is permissible unless proven to be prohibited, except in the case of acts of worship. Since entertainment in itself is not an act of worship, these new methods are permissible unless proven otherwise; it does not matter if the disbelievers discovered them first.

Chapter Six

Technology

*S*ince we are discussing the issue of alternatives, we must consider the technology that will be used. Technology in itself is permissible, and technological advancement is desirable for Muslims. However, the manner in which a gadget is used can make it ḥarâm. For example, it is permissible to use a mobile phone, but it is ḥarâm to use it for an illicit relationship. The following gadgets need some explanation on their usage.

Television

The most common tool of entertainment in the world today is the television. Even the poorest of people have a television set in their homes. It is a powerful tool that can be used for both good and evil; it is highly influential and plays a major role in shaping people's personalities and morals.

However, since its invention, the television has been used mainly as an instrument of the devil; it has been condemned completely by most Muslim scholars since it has proved more harmful than beneficial. It is only recently that Muslims have decided to use the television to propagate Islam and its teachings. As a result, it has been discovered that Muslims lack media content as compared to the disbelievers.

Shaykh Salman al-Oudah explains this change of opinion as follows:

> Other Islamic workers rejected mass media. They warned against the evils and the dangers of television. Alas, they ultimately found themselves compelled to accept the fact that such things were here to stay and could not be ignored. They realized that they were going to have to use the media to call people to Islam and give the people a wholesome alternative to the filth that they were watching. In this way, the television and other mass media options became means of disseminating Islam. These means were understood to take the ruling of the ends for which they were employed. They were not to be regarded as good and evil in and of themselves.[27]

Originally, Muslim scholars rejected television because it enabled many forms of immorality to enter the Muslim home and corrupt it from within. The effects of this are evident in many Muslim homes today, where there is unrestricted access to television programmes with unsuitable content.

However, scholars later realised the mistake of this ruling. It is not the television itself that is evil; instead, the way it is used determines whether it is good or evil. If television is being used correctly, it can be a great means of influencing people in the right direction. Taking this into consideration, many scholars have changed their rulings regarding television. It is a tool of mass communication, but it is the content that determines which of the five categories of fiqh it falls into. For example, watching women dressed in a sexually provocative manner would be harâm, while watching an Islamic lecture might be recommended.

A Muslim, however, should tread very carefully because most of what is shown on television is ḥarâm. It is best for Muslims to ensure that they tune in only to Islamic television stations and maintain a library of ḥalâl videos. Having un-Islamic television stations in the home can prove to be too difficult a test for many Muslims and their children.

Internet

The most powerful tool of mass communication and globalisation is the Internet. It has made an unlimited amount of information available at one's fingertips, but unfortunately, a great amount of evil is also accessible. The Internet is perhaps the toughest tool to pass a ruling on. On one hand, so much good has come out of it: many Islamic websites exist, online universities and programmes have been initiated, and people have reverted to Islam online. In short, the benefits of the Internet are too many to count.

On the other hand, a lot of evil has spread through the Internet, the most common of which is the widespread and easily accessible pornography, and the worst of which are the misleading websites that take people away from Islam. Many websites twist the teachings of Islam to make it look evil, and this is nothing but a trap of Satan to make Muslims apostatise. Many of these misleading websites are easily accessible, causing a great test for a Muslim's faith.

The Internet is like a minefield in which you must tread very carefully. You should fear Allah (ﷻ) and use it only for good. If you fear that you will not be able to use it for constructive purposes, then you should not install an Internet connection in your home. The following steps can help a person benefit from the Internet and avoid the traps of Satan:

1. Start by saying *Bismillâh* (In the name of Allah). If you begin using the Internet by remembering Allah (ﷻ), you will only use it for permissible purposes inshallah. A God-

fearing Muslim would not use the Internet for evil after taking Allah's name prior to using it.

2. Firmly resolve to use the Internet only for that which is beneficial. Ask Allah (ﷻ) to protect you from Satan and to guide you to the straight path. Your intention will help you to choose good websites, and your supplication will be a means of gaining Allah's protection from misinformation from Satan.

3. Make use of all the safety features available on your computer to block out pornographic and other unsuitable content.

4. The computer with Internet access should be in an open area of the house, where other members of the family can see what is being viewed. This will reduce the user's desire to access sinful content on it.

Mobile phones

The use of mobile phones has become so widespread that almost every child owns one. Furthermore, the mobile phone has become so technologically advanced that it has the features of a computer, television, radio and phone all in one. This has been the cause of great trials for Muslims. The phone has given young Muslims access to the opposite sex and to pornography and other evils, right in the palm of their hands. It is now possible for a young man to exchange text messages with a girlfriend while he is sitting at the same table as his parents, without them even knowing.

The question that needs to be raised is whether the phone is necessary. Why does a ten-year-old or a fourteen-year-old need a mobile phone? The phone does not contain many benefits for them; in contrast, the harms and temptations greatly outweigh the benefits. It is for this reason that I hold the opinion that it is not permissible for parents to hand over a mobile phone to their young children until they are mature, strong and spiritually developed enough to resist its evil temptations and to use it only for ḥalâl purposes. If this is not considered, then parents should not be surprised to find their children in illicit relationships.

A general rule for technology

Technology is like any other tool; it can be used for good or evil. It is up to the user to fear Allah (ﷻ) and to use His gifts in a way that pleases Him. A user who falls into error should repent and not allow the devil to overcome him or her. This is the balanced method; to completely cut Muslims off from technology would stifle the growth of Islam and any chance of Muslims becoming a rival to the West.

We must embrace and master technology, and then go on to develop more beneficial ways to use it. This will prove crucial to the development and growth of the Muslims, and it is definitely critical for the establishment of a Muslim state.

Chapter Seven

Misunderstood concepts

*T*here are a few misunderstood concepts with regard to Islam's stance on entertainment that have led people to adopt one of two extremes related to it. Inshallah in this chapter we will cover the most common misconceptions.

Religion is easy

As mentioned towards the beginning of this book, Islam is an easy religion to follow. It has few rules, and they are practical. Allah (🕮) has declared plenty of things to be lawful. Unfortunately, many Muslims stretch this concept beyond its limits and use it as an excuse to indulge in sinful forms of entertainment. It is common to find Muslims intermingling and enjoying themselves with sinful speech and pursuits, then saying to one who tries to correct them: "Islam is easy. Why are you making things difficult?"

The truth is that Islam is an easy religion, as mentioned in the Qur'an. However, the context of this is that Islam is easy to follow only if one makes an effort, and that it does not require anything that is beyond human capability. This does not mean that Islam has no limits and one is free to do as one pleases. Islam has boundaries, limits, rules and principles, all of which must be abided by, yet none of these are overbearing or beyond our capabilities. This is the correct understanding of this fundamental principle of Islam.

Allah's forgiveness

Many Muslims use Allah's attributes of forgiveness and mercy to indulge in sins and ḥarâm forms of entertainment. Their excuse is that Allah (﷾) is Most Forgiving and Most Merciful and will forgive them. They also claim that because they are Muslims, they will enter paradise and Allah (﷾) will forgive them; they use this as a further excuse to indulge in sins.

It is true that Allah (﷾) is the Most Forgiving and Most Merciful, but it should be noted that only Allah (﷾) can choose whom He will forgive and whom He will punish. The recognition of this reality will cause the believing slaves to do whatever good they can and to repent for their sins in order to try and earn Allah's mercy and forgiveness. Indeed, Allah (﷾) has promised to forgive His sincere worshippers and grant them paradise through His mercy.

Furthermore, a Muslim does not have an automatic guarantee of being granted entrance into paradise. True faith is manifest only through our actions, upon which we will be judged. Allah (﷾) has set the rules and conditions to enter paradise. We cannot fool Allah (﷾) or try to take advantage of His mercy and forgiveness to get what we desire in both the worlds. Allah (﷾) knows what is in our hearts and has every right to throw us in the hellfire if we harbour such thoughts.

Religious innovation (*bid'ah*)

There are some people who misunderstand the prohibition of religious innovation, using it as an excuse to turn the lawful into the unlawful and vice versa. One can find such people prohibiting

Islamic nasheed events, fairs, videos, conferences and the use of microphones during prayers on the pretext that since the Prophet (ﷺ) never did this, it must be an innovation. Some of these people also go to the extreme of prohibiting the use of chairs, high toilets and dining tables because the Prophet (ﷺ) did not use them.

The term 'bid'ah' refers to innovation in the religion. This means to invent an act of worship not performed by the Prophet (ﷺ) or to perform an act of worship in a manner different from his. It refers solely to acts of worship. This brings us back to the general ruling in Islam that all acts of worship are prohibited except those the Prophet (ﷺ) taught, while all things of this world are permissible unless prohibited by the Qur'an or Sunnah.

Since sitting on a chair, dining at a table and using the microphone are worldly acts, as are playing soccer, video games and singing, they are in themselves permissible unless explicitly prohibited. However, one can still argue that propagating Islam is an act of worship, and the Prophet (ﷺ) did not do it through videos, Internet or radio. While this is true, the reason behind it is that the technology to do these things did not exist in his time. He used every means of communication available during his time to spread the word of Islam, and he encouraged his followers to do the same.

Based upon this, it is permissible to use any means of communication available to us to spread the message of Islam, including video, radio, the Internet and the telephone. None of this can be considered an innovation in the religion.

Imitating the disbelievers

Some people prohibit the use of technology; the hosting of conferences, dinners and fairs; and the playing of sports, among other things, because they claim these things were invented by the disbeliever, and we are prohibited from imitating the disbelievers in any way. For proof, they quote the following hadith:

The Prophet (ﷺ) said: « Whoever imitates a people will be regarded as one of them. » (A sound hadith recorded by Abu Dâwood and Ibn Ḥibbân)

The hadith is authentic, but an explanation is necessary. This hadith cannot possibly mean that Muslims cannot do a single thing that the disbelievers also do. Cars, planes, supermarkets and many other things that we use daily were invented by the disbelievers, yet it is commonly accepted that such things are not prohibited.

Imitation of disbelievers can be categorised as follows:

1. Imitation in religion: This category is clearly prohibited and refers mainly to imitating the disbelievers in aspects which are specific to their religions. Examples of this include wearing the religious dress of any religion, celebrating birthdays (a practice that has its roots in Greek paganism), celebrating the birthday of our Prophet (which is an imitation of Christmas), using rosary beads for counting (which is an imitation of a Christian practice) and wearing a wedding ring on the ring finger of the left hand (which is a Christian religious practice). All of these are prohibited in Islam.

   The prohibition of this category can be concluded from a number of hadiths, the most famous of which is the Prophet's dislike of fasting on the day of 'Âshoorah alone since that was the religious practise of the Jews.

2. Imitation in that which is prohibited: This is clear because such a thing will be prohibited whether the disbelievers do it or not. A good example of this category is the prohibition of shaving the beard. Many Muslims today shave their beards to imitate men in the West, but this is the very reason the Prophet (ﷺ) gave for prohibiting it:

« Act against the polytheists, trim closely the moustache and grow the beard. » (Muslim)

3. Imitation in permissible worldly acts: The ruling on such things depends on one's intention. If people do the act because they like it or find it beneficial, then there is no harm in this. However, if they do it with the intention of imitating the disbelievers, then it becomes ḥarâm. The reason is that such an intention shows an inferiority complex to, and admiration for, the disbelievers, and this is completely ḥarâm. In such a case, the intention – rather than the act itself – is ḥarâm. The Prophet (ﷺ) said: « Every act is judged by its intention. » (Bukhari)

The reason for the permissibility is the fact that if we had to regard as prohibited everything the disbelievers do, this would be very impractical and would make life difficult. Islam is not against technological, social or scientific progress, and there is nothing wrong with using the same things that the disbelievers use. The following hadith further proves this:

The Prophet (ﷺ) said: « I intended to prohibit intercourse with a wife who was breastfeeding, but I remembered that the Greeks and Persians do that without causing any injury to their children. » (Muslim and Mâlik)

In this narration, the Prophet (ﷺ) mentioned that he was going to prohibit something, but then, after he saw the disbelievers doing it without harming themselves, he did not prohibit it. This is clear evidence for the permissibility of some worldly acts that the disbelievers do.

Detachment from the world (*zuhd*)

Zuhd refers to the Islamic concept of detaching your heart from this world. Unfortunately, there is a misconception that zuhd means abstaining from the permissible things of this world and being engaged in worship all the time. This unrealistic approach to Islam goes against the fiṭrah and chases people away from Islam because it is too extreme for most people to handle.

This attitude existed during the time of the Prophet (ﷺ). He refuted it and taught that it is not the way of Islam to go to such extremes and place unbearable hardships upon oneself. The following incident is proof of this:

« A group of three men came to the houses of the Prophet's wives, asking how the Prophet (ﷺ) worshipped [Allah (ﷺ)]. When they were informed about that, they considered their worship insufficient and said: Where are we in relation to the Prophet, as his past and future sins have been forgiven? Then one of them said: I will offer the prayer throughout the night forever. Another said: I will fast throughout the year and will not break my fast. The third said: I will keep away from the women and will never marry. Allah's Messenger (ﷺ) came to them and said: Are you the same people who said such-and-such? By Allah, I am more submissive to Allah and more afraid of Him than you; yet, I fast and break my fast, I do sleep and I also marry women. Whoever does not follow my Sunnah [way] is not from me [not one of my followers]. » (Bukhari)

In this narration, we find some Companions wanting to give up the permissible enjoyments of this world to a degree that is unnatural, intending to please Allah (ﷺ). This angered the Prophet (ﷺ), who always emphasised balance and moderation. Thus, it is not part of Islam to give up – or force others to give up – the permissible acts of this world to an unnatural and unhealthy extent. The Prophet (ﷺ) ate, drank and married women. He would also run races, ride horses and host wrestling matches between his Companions (may Allah be pleased with them). A person who shuns all of this in the name of Islam has in fact digressed from the way of Muhammad (ﷺ).

Conclusion

$\mathcal{I}$n the preceding pages, we have covered the basic rulings regarding entertainment in Islam, outlined the principles by which one can deduce specific rulings, listed the prohibited forms of entertainment and defined the recommended ones.

To conclude, we should remind ourselves to fear Allah (ﷻ) and remember that He created us to worship Him. Knowing that, we should not allow anything to distract us from His worship. At the same time, we should maintain a balance between enjoying Allah's bounties on this earth and worshipping Him. We should realise that any form of entertainment that distracts people from their duties to Allah (ﷻ) and their responsibilities to others becomes ḥarâm, even if it is generally permissible or recommended.

Allah (ﷻ) has prescribed for us a balanced religion, in tune with our fiṭrah. He has made it easy for anyone who makes an effort to practice it. We should stay away from the ḥarâm and everything that we consider doubtful. Instead, we should fulfil the obligations that Allah (ﷻ) has prescribed for us. This is the minimum requirement for a believer, and I ask Allah (ﷻ) to always keep us all firmly upon the straight path, protect us from the deceptions and distractions of the devil and make us the flag-bearers of the truth.

O Allah (ﷺ)! Send your peace and blessings upon the final Prophet (ﷺ) and all those who follow his way until the last day. All praise belongs only to Allah (ﷺ), the Lord of the worlds.

Notes

Introduction

[1] Muhammad Salih al-Munajjid, *The Muslim Home: 40 Recommendations in the Light of the Qur'an and Sunnah* (Riyadh: International Islamic Publishing House, 2005), 59.

[2] The translations of the meanings of the Qur'anic verses in this book have been taken from: Ṣaḥeeḥ International, *The Qur'an: Arabic Text with Corresponding English Meaning* (Jeddah: Abul Qâsim Publishing House, 1997).

Chapter 1

[3] Ibn Qayyim al-Jawziyah, *Al-Fawâ'id* (Egypt: Umm Al-Qura Al-Mansura, 2004).

[4] al-Munajjid, *The Muslim Home*, 61.

Chapter 3

[5] al-Jawziyah, *Al-Fawâ'id*.

[6] A battle that was fought before Islam between the Khazraj and the Aws tribes of the Anṣâr [the Muslim citizens of Madinah who gave refuge to the Prophet (ﷺ) and the other Muslim emigrants from Makkah].

[7] Imam Abu Hamid al-Ghazâli, *Ihyâ' 'Uloom ad-Deen*, 5:166. An English translation is available at: http://www.ghazali.org/articles/gz-music.pdf.

Chapter 4

[8] Recommended books on this topic are *The Fundamentals of Tawheed* by Dr. Abu Ameenah Bilal Philips and *Kitâb at-Tawheed* by Muhammad ibn Abdul-Wahhab.

[9] The Hindi-language film industry, centred in Mumbai, India (which was previously called Bombay). [Editor]

[10] Dr. Abu Ameenah Bilal Philips, *The Moral Foundations of Islamic Culture* (Available at: http://www.islamiconlineuniversity.com), 19.

[11] Hâkim has graded this hadith authentic, based on the endorsement of both Bukhari and Muslim.

[12] 'Abdullâh ibn Ahmad Ibn Qudâmah, *Al-Mughni: Sharh Al-Kabeer* (Cairo: Dar El Hadith, 1998), 10:171.

[13] Abu Zakariyâ Muhyi ad-Deen ibn Sharaf An-Nawawi, *Saheeh Muslim bi Sharh an-Nawawi* (Ad-Dirâsah: Dâr Abi Hiyân, 1995), 15:15.

[14] Imam Zaki ud-Deen 'Abdul-'Adheem al-Mundhiri, *At-Targheeb wat-Tarheeb min al-Hadeeth ash-Shareef* (Beirut: Dar Ibn Hazm, n.d.), 4:4.

[15] Dr. Abu Ameenah Bilal Philips, *The Purpose of Creation* (Riyadh: International Islamic Publishing House, 2005), 37.

[16] Ibn Taymiyah recorded this anecdote in *As-Sârim al-Maslool 'alâ Man Shatama ar-Rasool*, vol. 1, p. 31, but he neither authenticated it nor referenced its source. (Editor)

[17] Muhammad ibn 'Ali ash-Shawkhâni, *Ibtâl Da'watul Ijmâ' 'alâ Tahreem Mutlaqis Simâ* (n.d), 59.

[18] Ibid., 52.

[19] Taqi ud-Deen Abul-'Abbâs Ibn Taymiyah, *Majmoo' al-Fatâwâ* (Cairo: Al-Maktabât at-Tawfiqiyyah), 5:566.

[20] Imam Abu Bakr al-Bayhaqi, *As-Sunan Al-Kubra* (Beirut: Dar al-Kutub al- Ῑlmiyah, n.d), 9:234.

[21] Mâlik ibn Anas, *Al-Muwaṭṭâ* (Karachi: Nurmuhammad Kutub Khana, n.d.), vol. 52:2, p. 7.

[22] Ḥâkim has graded this hadith authentic, based on the endorsement of both Bukhari and Muslim.

Chapter 5

[23] Ibn Qayyim al-Jawziyah, *Madârij as-Sâlikeen* (California: Dar al-Kitab al-Arabi, 2004), 2:26.

[24] The tenth day of the Islamic month of Muḥarram; it is recommended that Muslims fast on this day to commemorate the victory of Prophet Moosâ (ﷺ) over the Pharaoh.

[25] Aḥmad ibn 'Ali Ibn Ḥajar al-'Asqalâni, *Fatḥ al-Bâri Sharḥ Ṣaḥeeḥ al-Bukhâri* (Riyadh: Darussalam, 2000), 10:543.

[26] Nâṣiruddin al-Albâni, *Âdâb az-Zafâf* (Egypt: Dar as-Salâm, 2002), 196.

Chapter 6

[27] Salman al-Oudah, *Walking the Straight Path: Constancy, Renewal and the Contemporary Muslim,* accessed January 15, 2011, http://www.islamkenya.com/html/ebooks.html, 2.

Bibliography

al-Albâni, Nâṣiruddin. *Âdâb az-Zafâf.* Egypt: Dar as-Salâm, 2002.

al-Bayhaqi, Imam Abu Bakr. *As-Sunan Al-Kubra.* Beirut: Dar al-Kutub al-Ilmiyah, n.d.

al-Bukhari, Muhammad ibn Ismʻaeel. *Ṣaḥeeḥ al-Bukhâri.* Karachi: Qadimi Kutub Khana, n.d.

al-Ghazâli, Imam Abu Hamid. *Iḥyâ' 'Uloom ad-Deen.* Accessed January 15, 2011. http://www.ghazali.org/articles/gz-music.pdf.

Ibn Anas, Mâlik. *Al-Muwaṭṭâ.* Karachi: Nurmuhammad Kutub Khana, n.d.

Ibn Ḥajar al-ʻAsqalâni, Aḥmad ibn 'Ali. *Fatḥ al-Bâri Sharḥ Ṣaḥeeḥ al-Bukhâri.* Riyadh: Darussalam, 2000.

Ibn Kathir, Ismâʻeel. *Tafsir Ibn Kathir.* Riyadh: Darussalam, 2002.

Ibn Qudâmah, 'Abdullâh ibn Aḥmad. *Al-Mughni: Sharh Al-Kabeer.* Cairo: Dar El Hadith, 1998.

Ibn Taymiyah, Taqi ud-Deen Abul-'Abbâs. *Majmooʻ al-Fatâwâ.* Cairo: Al Maktabât at-Tawfiqiyyah, n.d.

al-Jawziyah, Ibn Qayyim. *Al-Fawâ'id.* Egypt: Umm Al-Qura Al-Mansura, 2004.

——. *Madârij as-Sâlikeen.* California: Dar al-Kitab al-Arabi, 2004.

al-Kanadi,AbuBilalMustafa. *TheIslamicRulingonMusicandSinging.* Makkah: Bilal M. Al-Kanadi and Brothers, 1998.

Khan, Dr. Muhammad Muhsin and Dr. Muhammad Taqi-ud-Din al-Hilali. *Translation of the Meaning of the Noble Quran.* Riyadh: Darussalam, 1996.

Malik, Muhammad Farooq-e-Azam. *Al-Qur'an: The Guidance for Mankind.* Houston, Texas: The Institute of Islamic Knowledge, 2006.

MSA West, *Hadith Database.* Accessed January 15, 2011. http:// msawest.net/islam.

al-Munajjid, Muhammad Salih. *Muharramât: Forbidden Matters Some People Take Lightly.* Riyadh: International Islamic Publishing House, 2004.

——. *The Muslim Home: 40 Recommendations in the Light of the Qur'an and Sunnah.* Riyadh: International Islamic Publishing House, 2005.

al-Mundhiri, Imam Zaki ud-Deen 'Abdul-'Adheem. *At-Targheeb wat-Tarheeb min al-Hadeeth ash-Shareef.* Beirut: Dar Ibn Hazm.

Muslim, Ibn al-Hajjâj. *Saheeh Muslim.* Karachi: Qadimi Kutub Khana, n.d.

an-Nawawi, Abu Zakariyâ Muhyi ad-Deen ibn Sharaf. *Saheeh Muslim bi Sharh an-Nawawi.* Ad-Dirâsah: Dâr Abi Hiyân, 1995.

al-Oudah, Salman. *Walking the Straight Path: Constancy, Renewal and the Contemporary Muslim.* Accessed January 15, 2011. http://www.islamkenya.com/html/ebooks.html.

Philips, Dr. Abu Ameenah Bilal. *The Evolution of Fiqh.* Riyadh: International Islamic Publishing House, 2005.

——. *The Fundamentals of Tawheed: Islamic Monotheism.* Riyadh: International Islamic Publishing House, 2005.

——. *The Moral Foundations of Islamic Culture* (Available at: http://www.islamiconlineuniversity.com)

——. *The Purpose of Creation*. Riyadh: International Islamic Publishing House, 2005.

al-Qaradâwi, Dr. Yusuf. *The Lawful and Prohibited in Islam*. Cairo: Al-Falah Foundation, 2001.

as-Sajistâni,AbuDâwood.*SunanAbuDâwood*.Karachi:QadimiKutub Khana, n.d.

ash-Shawkâni,Muḥammadibn'Ali.*IbtâlDa'watulIjmâ''alâTaḥreem Mutlaqis Simâ*, n.d.

at-Tirmidhi, Abu 'Eesâ. *Jâmi' at-Tirmidhi*. Karachi: Qadimi Kutub Khana, n.d.

Wayhaqih, Abdur Rahman ibn Mu'allal. *Al-Ghulu fid-Deen*. Beirut, Lebanon: Reṣalâh Publishers, 2002.

Appendix

$\mathcal{J}$ have decided to include at the end of this book an article on entertainment that I originally wrote for my blog. Since this article was written for a blog and aimed at a younger audience, the style is casual and different in tone from the rest of this book.

This article has been written for younger readers. Parents who have read this book, but are having difficulty getting their teenagers to read it, can refer them to this appendix, inshallah, for a fun look at this topic.

Top Ten Forms of Halal Entertainment
By Abu Muawiyah Ismail Kamdar

Many Muslims hold a misconception that having fun is ḥarâm. Nothing could be further from the truth. Having fun is part of human nature, and Islam is the religion of fiṭrah (human nature). Unfortunately, despite the fact that most forms of entertainment are ḥalâl, many Muslims seem to indulge in the ḥarâm forms instead. Here are my top ten favourite ḥalâl things to do for fun. However, do remember that even ḥalâl forms of entertainment become ḥarâm through overindulgence and neglecting one's Islamic duties.

10. Eating out

Everybody enjoys going out to their favorite fast food joint and enjoying a delicious chicken tikka or burger. This is completely ḥalâl and extremely fun, especially when you go with company. So go ahead and enjoy yourself, but just make sure the chicken is ḥalâl. ;-)

9. Reading

Not everybody enjoys this, but I do. There's nothing like a good book to take your mind off things and help you relax. Of course, you must choose a book whose content is ḥalâl. It is preferable to read books by Muslims unless you have reached the level of knowledge to read books by non-Muslim authors and be able to separate the good from the evil. Don't forget that the first command in the Qur'an was to 'read'. Enjoy your reading, and may Allah (ﷻ) help us all reach the level where we enjoy reading Islamic books.

8. Swimming

This one has been recommended by the Prophet (ﷺ), and there's no better way to cool off on a hot day! So make sure your body is covered appropriately, and enjoy the water this summer.

7. Relaxing

We all need a break, and nobody can pray all day. The Prophet (ﷺ) recommended that we live our lives in balance and said:

« There is a time for this and a time for that. » (Muslim)

This essentially means that we should split our day and strike a balance between Islamic work and living life. So don't stress when you get tired; just sit back and relax. It's perfectly ḥalâl! Just don't sleep through any prayer times.

6. Video games and videos

Not all video games and videos are ḥarâm; it is the content that matters. If you enjoy playing video games and can balance it with other duties without getting addicted, then go ahead. However, do make sure you only buy ḥalâl games. (That means no Grand Theft Auto!) The same goes for movies and other videos. Watch something Islamic or beneficial. Keep away from movies that have shameless scenes and teach inappropriate things.

Most importantly, don't get addicted and sit till the time of the dawn prayer playing Pro Evolution Soccer, because that would then become ḥarâm. Strike a balance! Be careful and responsible when choosing the content, and don't try to fool yourself that a certain movie is ḥalâl when you know it's not, because you can't fool Allah (﷾) or the angels who are sitting with you, watching every moment and writing everything down in your book of deeds.

5. Nature

I love nature! Whether it's the ocean, forests, or animals, I just love being out in the natural environment. It's one of the times when I feel most peaceful and close to Allah (﷾). There is no feeling equal to praying under a tree or on a mountain. Take my word for it and book your next family holiday at a place of natural beauty like the Drakensburg Mountains of South Africa. It is beautiful!

4. Nasheeds

I love nasheeds. In them, I have found the perfect replacement for music and a source of both joy and education for myself. It was narrated that Umar (﷜) said: "Singing is the companion of the traveller." I don't know how authentic that narration is, but Imam Mâlik did say that there's nothing wrong with singing while travelling, so load your cars with CDs of Zain Bhikha and Dawud

Wharnsby. Throw out the harâm music and enjoy halâl, beneficial entertainment as you drive to work and back.

3. Hanging out with the right crowd

Your friends either make you or break you. The Prophet (ﷺ) said: « Every person follows the religion of his best friend, so be careful whom you befriend. » (A reliable hadith recorded by Ahmad, Abu Dâwood and at-Tirmidhi)

Since we are all social beings, hanging out and socialising is high on our list of ways to have fun. Yet it is very important to have the right friends. Your friends are the ones who encourage you either to pray or to skip the prayer and catch a movie. They are the ones who tell you either that your hijâb looks beautiful or it makes you look old. In the end, who you choose to hang out with will make the biggest difference in who you become.

2. Playing with kids

I have two baby boys, two baby nieces, a baby brother, a baby cousin and many other little people in the family. There is nothing more fun for me than spending time with these innocent, sweet kids and playing with them. Children are a joy and the coolness of my eyes. On this point, I hate people who cannot stand kids and treat them badly. It is because of such people in our mosques that many kids grow up traumatised and hate the mosque in particular and Islam in general. That is not Islamic at all.

The Prophet (ﷺ) would play with kids even in the mosque. Sometimes he would prolong his prostration because his grandchildren were riding on his back. That is the Sunnah! The Sunnah is not to ban the kids from the mosque and growl at them whenever you see them! Playing with children is one of the Sunnah methods of having fun.

« Abu Hurayrah (🙵) reported: The Prophet (🙵) kissed his grandson, Ḥasan ibn 'Ali, in the presence of Aqra' ibn Habis. Thereupon, Aqra' remarked: I have ten children, and I have never kissed any of them. The Messenger of Allah (🙵) cast a glance upon him and said: He who does not show mercy to others will not be shown mercy. » (Bukhari and Muslim)

Think about that the next time you are unkind to a child.

1. Marriage and all the fun it legalises

Being with the opposite gender is the natural desire of every human. In such a situation, one has the most fun, especially if the two are in love. Islam does not prohibit this but promotes it in the form of marriage; it prohibits it only outside of marriage. So dump your boyfriends and girlfriends, get religious and marry a cool religious person!

The Prophet (🙵) stressed the importance of marriage many times and also stressed the importance of having a fun marriage. If your marital life sucks, your life in general will be miserable. However, if you are happily married and enjoying it (like I am) then you can cope with every other problem you face. The Prophet (🙵) had fun in his marital life; he raced with his wives, joked with them, and even was known to have joined in a food fight with them once. Study his life with them; he was the perfect husband, so let us all follow in his footsteps.

The Prophet (🙵) once told a young Companion who had married an older, previously-married woman: « Why haven't you married a virgin who would have played with you, and you would have played with her? » (Bukhari)

So what are you waiting for? If you're married, improve the quality of your marital life and make it a source of fun and pleasure for yourself. If you're not married, get married soon and have lots of kids so that you can then do everything else on this list with your wife and kids. It's more fun than when you are alone.

I hope you all enjoyed and benefitted from this list. I also hope that it will assist you in living ḥalâl, practising Islam and enjoying it. May Allah (﷾) guide us all to the straight and balanced path and put the love of Islam into our hearts. *Âmeen* (Amen).

Glossary of Islamic Terms*

abu (or *abi*)	أبو ، أبي	father (of)
alḥamdulillâh	الحمد لله	all praise is for Allah
âmeen	آمين	O Allah, accept our invocation; amen
angel	ملاك	A being made of light who is totally obedient to Allah and has no free will; Allah has assigned some angels specific tasks, like those who record our good and bad deeds, the Angel of Death, the guardians of hell, etc.
banu (or *bani*)	بنو ، بني	*lit.* 'children (of)'; usu. referring to a tribe that claims a common ancestor
bid'ah	بدعة	innovation, esp. undesired innovation in matters of religion

---

* The Arabic words are transliterated according to the conventions of the Transliteration Chart found in this book. If a word has become part of the English language (that is, is found in a dictionary of Standard English), that spelling is used in this book and appears first in this Glossary, with the transliterated form in brackets after it.

bismillâh	بسم الله	in the name of Allah
deen	دين	religion
Eid ('eed)	عيد	*lit.* festival; the two celebrations: one at the end of Ramadan and the other at the culmination of the Hajj
farḍ	فرض	compulsory
fiqh	فقه	Islamic jurisprudence; understanding or interpreting Islamic law
fiṭrah	فطرة	the natural inclination (of humans) instilled by Allah
hadith (ḥadeeth)	حديث	a statement or action of Prophet Muhammad (ﷺ) that was remembered and recorded by his Companions and followers
halal (ḥalâl)	حلال	permitted according to Islamic law
ḥarâm	حرام	forbidden according to Islamic law
hijab (ḥijâb)	حجاب	veil ordained by Allah for believing women
'ibâdât (sg. 'ibâdah)	عبادات	acts of worship
ijmâ'	إجماع	consensus: a method of deriving rulings in jurisprudence
inshallah	أن شاءالله	God willing
kufr	الكفر	disbelief in Allah and/or what He has revealed

madh-hab (pl. *madhâhib*)	مذهب	school of juristic thought
makrooh	مكروه	disliked
mubâḥ	مباح	permissible
nasheed	نشيد	Islamic song
qiyâs	قياس	analogy: a method of deriving rulings in jurisprudence
Sharia (*shari'ah*)	شريعة	Islamic law derived from the Qur'an and the Sunnah
shaykh	شيخ	teacher, mentor; scholar
shirk	الشرك	associating partners with Allah
siḥr	سحر	magic
Sunnah	سنة	the practice and collected sayings of Prophet Muhammad (ﷺ) that together with the Qur'an forms the basis of Islamic law
sunnah	سنة	acts that are recommended but not mandatory
zinâ	زنى	adultery or fornication
zuhd	زهد	detachment from the material world